International Perspectives on Student Behavior

International Perspectives on Student Behavior

What We Can Learn

Charles J. Russo, Izak Oosthuizen, and
Charl C. Wolhuter

ROWMAN & LITTLEFIELD
Lanham • Boulder • New York • London

Published by Rowman & Littlefield
A wholly owned subsidiary of The Rowman & Littlefield Publishing Group, Inc.
4501 Forbes Boulevard, Suite 200, Lanham, Maryland 20706
www.rowman.com

Unit A, Whitacre Mews, 26-34 Stannery Street, London SE11 4AB

British Library Cataloguing in Publication Information Available

Library of Congress Cataloging-in-Publication Data

Library of Congress Cataloging-in-Publication Data Available
ISBN 978-1-4758-1482-8 (cloth : alk. paper) -- ISBN 978-1-4758-1483-5 (pbk. : alk. paper) -- ISBN 978-1-4758-1484-2 (electronic)

∞™ The paper used in this publication meets the minimum requirements of American National Standard for Information Sciences Permanence of Paper for Printed Library Materials, ANSI/NISO Z39.48-1992.

Printed in the United States of America

To our wives,
Debbie
Amori
Irené
With all of our love and affection

Contents

Preface

Charles J. Russo, Charl C. Wolhuter, and Izak Oosthuizen

A cornerstone for effective teaching and learning is vested in the quality of the way in which students focus on the content of their lessons.[1] Educational practitioners and academics agree that classroom order is a *sine qua non* for effective learning. A constant challenge for teachers and other educational leaders in seeking to maintain safe and orderly learning environments is the seemingly endless occurrences of student misconduct. Moreover, there appears to be a worldwide deterioration of student conduct in schools.

As the world becomes a global village, educators can learn from the experiences of colleagues in other nations who have had success in addressing issues of student discipline. Consequently, it is important for practitioners to uncover effective methods to deal with student misconduct. The objective of this book is to identify the best practices in ten nations on six continents for dealing with student misconduct in a legally sound manner.

It is a well-accepted and tested practice that when national education systems grapple with educational issues, comparative international perspectives can be reviewed for assistance. Put another way, when countries face particular educational issues or challenges, educators in one nation could benefit from the experience of their peers elsewhere who faced or are still facing similar concerns. The study of the experience of educators in other countries can reveal the full extent and implications of the problem and possible contributory causes while suggesting solutions for dealing with student misconduct. Against this background this volume offers the experience of ten countries in dealing with student misconduct in the hope that it will open a wider perspective to academics, policy makers, and educators alike, eventually making a contribution toward the successful dealing with student misconduct.

The chapters in this book offer cross-national perspectives on best practices when dealing with the challenge of student misconduct. The chapter authors, all distinguished academics or jurists, have contributed their reviews of the state of the law and practice in their nations. As readers peruse the chapters, they will recognize that the way in which educators address student discipline varies around the world.

As such, this is the fifth book in a series of volumes on comparative legal issues in education. The earlier volumes addressed the rights of students,[2] teachers,[3] and students with disabilities[4] in addition to the status of higher education.[5] The chapters on individual countries in this volume are Australia (Joan Squelch), Brazil (Nina Beatriz Stocco Ranieri), China (Ran Zhang, Jun Wang, and Suping Shen), Malaysia (Fatt Hee Tie), New Zealand (Sally Varnham), Singapore (Mui Kim Teh), South Africa (Marius H. Smit and J. P. Rossouw), Turkey (Ricardo Lozano and Irem Kizilaslan), United Kingdom (Patricia Walker), and United States (Charles J. Russo). The book rounds out with a chapter of analysis by the editors that draws on the issues raised throughout the book and centers on the concept of best practice management, ending with concrete suggestions aimed at improving educational practice.

The first book of its kind, and a companion volume to earlier comparative texts identified earlier, consists of a collection of essays designed to enhance a common understanding of the rights of students when they are subjected to discipline. As the world continues to shrink, and interdependence grows, a major challenge facing educators in the global community is ensuring the rights of students who are being disciplined while working to maintain order so that their other children can learn in safe and orderly school environments.

Readers are advised that insofar as each of the nations covered in this book uses slightly different systems of legal citation, we have left references in their original form rather than attempt to standardize them under one American rubric. Finally, we preserved minor variations in the different forms of English used globally so that readers can get a flavor of how this seemingly common tongue is used throughout the world, particularly for academics whose native language is not English.

Of course, no single book can ever hope to cover the myriad of legal topics, or laws of nations, addressing the legal status of discipline in schools. Even so, we hope that these informative, thought-provoking, well-written, and researched chapters, authored by leading academics or jurists in the field, can serve as up-to-date and ready sources of information to help keep educational leaders, academics, and students abreast of the many changes in the ever-growing area of comparative student discipline.

NOTES

1. For the sake of consistency, this book usually refers to children in K–12 schools as students. Even so, the authors recognize that other nations use different terms. For example, educators in South Africa tend to speak of "learners," while those in the United Kingdom typically refer to "pupils." Thus, we have left these variations in place rather than seek to standardize the use of terminology.

2. Charles J. Russo, Jan DeGroof, and Douglas J. Stewart, eds., *The Educational Rights of Students: International Perspectives on Demystifying the Legal Issues* (Lanham, MD: Rowman and Littlefield Education, 2007).

3. Charles J. Russo and Jan DeGroof, eds., *The Employment Rights of Teachers: Exploring Education Law Worldwide* (Lanham, MD: Rowman and Littlefield Education, 2009).

4. Charles J. Russo, ed., *The Legal Rights of Students with Disabilities: International Perspectives* (Lanham, MD: Rowman and Littlefield Education, 2011).

5. Charles J. Russo, ed., *Handbook of Comparative Higher Education Law* (Lanham, MD: Rowman and Littlefield Education, 2011).

Acknowledgments

As with any book, there are a number of people who must be thanked. Four sets of people were very helpful in helping put this book together. First, many thanks to Tom Koerner, vice president and editorial director at Rowman and Littlefield Education, who was most supportive of this project from its inception through publication. Thanks also to Carlie Wall, associate editor, Chris Basso, production editor, and Crystal Clifton for copyediting the text.

Second, it almost goes without saying that we are grateful to the authors for their valuable contributions to this book.

Third, we would like to thank Charlie's assistant, Elizabeth Pearn at the University of Dayton, for her efforts in copyediting and helping to prepare the final manuscript for publication.

Fourth, but certainly not least, we would like to express our deepest appreciation for our wives, Debbie, Amori, and Irené, to whom this book is dedicated, for their ongoing love and support, without which none of this work would have been completed.

Introduction

The objective of this second volume of companion books on comparative student discipline is to identify the best practices in dealing with student misconduct on six continents in a legally sound manner. It is essential for educators to examine national as well as international practices addressing student misconduct in schools because learner misbehavior often has a detrimental effect on the quality of teaching and learning in elementary and secondary schools.

The essence of order in school environments can hardly be overemphasized. In the context of teaching-learning, order is to be regarded as a *sine qua non* (an indispensable condition) for effective learning. One of the cornerstones for effective teaching and learning is vested in the extent to which students can focus on the content of lessons. Interruptions as a result of student noise such as talking during lessons, or when learners constantly interrupt teachers, can upset the focus of an entire class.

This book is designed to show how learner misconduct calls for global awareness and collaboration. It is important to study this issue because not only are everyday trivial disturbances in class problems, but from media reports incidents of serious misconduct are increasing. In fact, there have been multiple assaults and killing of learners and teachers on school premises. Moreover, the latter constitute more than mere misconduct, they are acts of criminal misbehavior.

When student misbehavior turns into serious misconduct and ultimately criminal activity, alarms sound in the global community insofar as schools have sadly become danger instead of secure, tranquil environments enhancing teaching and learning. It is thus time to rethink strategies and approaches to learner discipline.

Educators can effectively learn from the experiences of peers in other countries, especially from their successes dealing with student misconduct. As such, this book endeavors to promote a global reciprocity as it examines causes, tendencies, and forms of misconduct in ten nations. Further, this book focuses on effective methods of dealing with student misconduct.

Following this brief introduction, which highlights key themes to be identified, the remainder of the book analyzes the detrimental effects of student misconduct on teaching and learning environments in schools.

MISCONDUCT HAMPERS TEACHING AND LEARNING

A constant encumbrance for order in teaching and learning environments is student misconduct. The Teaching and Learning International Survey, *Creating Effective Teaching and Learning Environments: First Results*, by the Organization for Economic Cooperation and Development (OECD Report),[1] highlighted international concern for studying the detrimental effects student misconduct is having on teaching and learning. The OECD report contained a comprehensive survey of ninety thousand teachers in twenty-three counties.

One of the findings of the OECD Report was that although positive school climates were associated with higher levels of student achievement, disruption of class instruction due to learner misconduct hinders the provision of proper instruction. As such, these disruptions have a detrimental effect on teaching and learning.

In addition to disturbances in the classrooms, which ranked first among the incidences of misconduct, the OECD Report ranked the other high frequented incidences of student misconduct as student absenteeism (46 percent); students arriving late at school (39 percent); profanity and swearing (37 percent); intimidation or verbal abuse of other students (35 percent); intimidation and verbal abuse of teachers and staff (17 percent); physical injury of other students (16 percent); theft (15 percent); possession of alcohol or drugs (11 percent).[2]

CONCERN FOR STUDENT SAFETY

Another important aspect which necessitates the proper handling of student misconduct refers to the safety of fellow learners and school staff. It is important that teachers respond immediately to minor incidents of misconduct before they can escalate into more serious difficulties that can pose a threat to the safety of school communities.

THE PROBLEM OF CRIMINAL TENDENCIES

It is critical that some forms of serious misconduct, such as the possession of drugs or weapons or assaults of teachers or peers, are criminal offenses. In perhaps the two worst examples of such behavior, at Columbine High School in Colorado and in Sandy Hook Elementary School in Newtown, Connecticut,[3] students went so far as attacking and killing other learners and peers. It goes without saying that tendencies such as these cannot be ignored nor go unpunished since remaining passive in the face of such behavior would actually be the same as condoning it. Further, tolerating these tendencies would constitute professional negligence.

DEALING WITH MISCONDUCT

In many schools worldwide, there appears to be a need for additional, legally sound methods to deal with student misconduct more effectively. Traditional methods applicable to typical student misconduct such as detention, the setting of school and classroom rules, demerit points, and corporal punishment (in some countries) are effectively applied in some situations but in others they prove to be less effective.

Many educational practitioners claim that the majority of these traditional methods are less effective while others argue that the application of corporal punishment proves to be one of the most effective methods in dealing with learner misconduct. Yet, in many countries corporal punishment in schools is regarded as unconstitutional or deemed to be inhuman and degrading.

DEALING WITH SERIOUS MISCONDUCT

A major problem actually lies with the serious forms of student misconduct. This leads to the following questions:

- How should teachers deal with serious forms of misconduct?
- What methods are available to deal effectively with student violence, theft, assault, and possession of drugs or dangerous weapons?
- What methods are utilized in ten countries on the six inhabited continents?
- Which of these methods are applied effectively?
- What other possible methods can be suggested or should be developed?

THE GLOBAL JOURNEY

In the quest to find answers to these questions, this book embarks on a tour through the global village. The remainder of this chapter provides a brief overview of dealing with learner misconduct in Brazil, China, Malaysia, South Africa, and Turkey.

In the state of São Paulo, Brazil, the emphasis falls on restorative justice where schools and the juvenile courts work in partnership. The National Education Act is protective rather than punitive. There is also a strong current of preventative actions whereby conflicts in schools and communities are resolved by mediators such that each school has its own professionally trained School and Community Mediator Teacher, acting to resolve conflict. Other successful programs include Prevention Can Be Taught, which endeavors to reduce student vulnerability to drugs, alcohol, and teenage pregnancy while Community Present promotes nonviolent conflict resolution.

Misconduct occurs in schools in China at a much more reduced rate than in the West. A survey in Beijing indicated that a vast majority of learners have never been subjected to disciplinary measures in part because Chinese culture is grounded in the Confucian philosophy of requiring students to obey their teachers, following their commands.

At the same time, learners in China seem to adhere to Max Weber's authority theories emanating charismatic authority versus a legally regulated dispensation. In terms of Weber's theories the relationship between student and teacher is one of a "father-son relationship," rather than one regulated by legal directives. Moreover, the notion of due process is relatively new in Chinese schools.

The Malaysian education system is relatively free from physical and emotional threats because their approach is much like that in Australia in the sense that educators focus on the *in loco parentis* role of the teacher. This common law role of the teacher affords them the right to maintain discipline to prevent students from becoming physical or emotional victims of the unruly behavior of peers. Overall, because the Malaysian approach to discipline adheres to the philosophy "to spare the rod would in turn spoil the child," strictly controlled corporal punishment is allowed in schools.

Learner misconduct in Turkey does not seem to be much of a problem and is trivial in nature: Talking in class counts among the most frequent forms of misconduct. In Turkey students are expected to obey teachers. In this regard, the chapter reports on a recent study which revealed that a significant majority of fifteen-year-old students in Turkey consider their classrooms to be calm environments. Although corporal punishment has been banned from schools, a majority of students continue to be subjected to a degree of corporal punishment. Further, as in other nations due process in schools is just about nonexistent.

Learner misconduct in South Africa is regulated by legislative provisions based on a progressive constitution. Since the promulgation of the South African Constitution in 1996, issues related to student misconduct such as freedom of expression, cultural and religious rights, the right to privacy, violence, sexual assault and assault in schools, the application of corporal punishment in schools, expulsion and suspension of learners as well as various aspects of administrative justice have been scrutinized in the South African High Court.

It is unfortunate that during the past twenty years the quality of education in public schools in South Africa has not improved and departmental administration has stumbled from one crisis to the next. Moreover, in many respects, learner conduct in public schools has taken a plunge.

CONCLUSION

The sound management of learner misconduct is essential for optimal teaching and learning. In many instances schools and societies lost track in dealing with learner misconduct to the detriment of orderly teaching and learning environments. In other settings it appears that school officials found the key to enhance positive student conduct to the best interest of the young.

All who are interested in education should seek to capture some of these successful strategies for application in their own challenging circumstances. The global overview of learner conduct in the following chapters provides a window of opportunity for reciprocity, there creating an option to exchange the pages from one another's experiences.

NOTES

1. Available at http://www.oecd.org/edu/school/43023606.pdf (OECD Report). *See also* http://www.oecd.org/edu/school/creatingeffectiveteachingandlearningenvironmentsfirstresults-fromtalis.htm.
2. Id. at 40.
3. For a commentary on this tragedy, see Charles J. Russo, "Armed Teachers and Guards Won't Make Schools Safer." *Education Week* 32(19) (2013): 27, 32.

Chapter One

Bringing Peace to Schools

The Experience of the State of São Paulo, Brazil

Nina Beatriz Stocco Ranieri

This chapter examines the State of São Paulo School Protection System (*Sistema de Proteção Escolar do Estado de São Paulo*, "the system"), an experience that has proven successful in promoting peace in public schools with high violence rates. The system was introduced in 2009 through interventions aimed at preventing criminal violence as well as any forms of symbolic verbal abuse, including bullying and intimidation, and the breaking of school rules. These interventions consist of different types of actions and approaches that vary according to the target audience and school facilities.

The interventions include, above all, so-called mediation and restorative justice practices, which are focused on solving conflicts through nonpunitive methods, as recommended by the United Nations Economic and Social Council.

In addressing the system, this chapter is divided into four parts. Part one introduces the Brazilian educational system from a legal perspective. The second section describes legal procedures under the Child and Adolescent Act and student misconduct. Part three presents the State of São Paulo School Protection System while the fourth section addresses the role of the School and Community Mediator Teacher in this system.

This chapter offers neither a complete analysis nor a conclusive solution to the problem of bringing peace to schools, but points out some of the facts that gave rise to the experience of preventing misconduct in schools, and from this viewpoint discusses the new roles that may be played by school officials.

THE BRAZILIAN EDUCATIONAL SYSTEM FROM A CONSTITUTIONAL PERSPECTIVE

In the Brazilian 1988 Constitution, the provisions concerning the right to education are found under Titles II and VIII, which concern fundamental rights and social organizations, respectively. As a fundamental right, education is ensured under Article 6 and defined under Article 205 as "a right for all and duty of the State and the family, promoted and fostered with the cooperation of society, aiming at the full development of the person, preparing the individual for the exercise of citizenship and training the individual for work." As such, the right to education is addressed at the same time as a long-, mid-, and short-term public policy that unfolds in rights and duties, binding obligations and restrictions.

Among all the social fundamental rights enshrined in the constitutional text, the right to education received the highest number of provisions: approximately fifty articles address the right to education directly and indirectly in terms of protecting, fostering, and ensuring the right to education. In comparing the amount of provisions governing the right to education to the number devoted to other equally important rights, such as health and social security, the latter are objects of nine and eight articles, respectively.

As a result, there is a complex system in place in Brazil to distribute lawmaking authority, duties, and income to the federal units such as the federation, states, municipalities, and the Federal District in order to fulfill the right to education. In doing so, the following features stand out: education in Brazil is organized collaboratively by the Federal government, the states, the municipalities, and the Federal District (Article 211); priorities are defined by law according to the level of education, in growing order of the scope of level of education (Article 211); the share of taxes to be applied to maintaining and developing education is established in statute (Article 212), this is an exception to the nonbinding allocation of taxes clause (Article 167, IV); and the law forbids taxes on the assets, income, or services of not-for-profit educational entities (Article 150, VI, c).

For children and adolescents, education is a right and a duty of the utmost priority (Article 227). For this reason, schooling is by law compulsory, universal, and free of charge, in addition to being considered a subjective right (Article 208, paragraph 1), including for those who did not have access to school at the appropriate age.

The Federal Constitution entitles all children in fundamental school from ages six to fourteen, at no cost to their parents or guardians, to be assisted by means of supplementary government programs providing school material, food, and health care. Government authorities and school officials cannot refrain from providing these services under the penalty of the law (Article 208).

Besides enjoying constitutional status, the right to education is protected and promoted, whether directly or indirectly, by the obligations set forth in international agreements to which Brazil is a signatory. Examples include the Universal Declaration of Human Rights (UDHR), the Convention against Discrimination in Education (Decree 36 223 of September 6, 1968), the International Covenant on Economic, Social and Cultural Rights (Decree 591, 1992), and the Convention on the Rights of the Child of 1989 (Decree 99 710 of November 21, 1990). At the regional level, the Brazilian legislature has adopted the Charter of the Organization of the American States (1948), the Pact of San Jose (1978) on civil and political rights, and the San Salvador Protocol (1988). These were thereby incorporated into Brazilian law in 1950, 1992, and 1996, respectively.

All the international instruments mentioned previously adopted UDHR general guidance to promote and protect the right to education, under the principles of diversity of means and identity of purpose which have marked international law as of the declaration. Therefore, the nature and content of education are determined based on United Nations goals, namely to promote human rights and peace plus the affirmation of free and democratic societies with the objective of building a universal, peaceful, and democratic culture.

The principles and norms of the international right to education are mirrored in the Brazilian Constitution just as the special features of this right like its legal nature, widespread entitlement, continuity, and nonexhaustive nature of its accessory obligations. More specifically, at the national level, overall guidelines to the implementation of the right to education are determined under the National Education Act (NEA) (Law 9394/1996), the National Education Plan (NEP) (Law 10 172/01) and under the Child and Adolescent Act (ECA) (Law 8 069/1990), among other federal laws.

The Implementation of the Right to Education Under Brazilian Law

The Brazilian educational system is decentralized and complex. Insofar as Brazil is a federation comprised of twenty-six states and more than 5,500 municipalities, the NEA divided Brazilian territory into three different categories of educational systems: the federal (which includes all the schools and universities maintained with federal resources, and also the private universities and colleges across the country); the state systems (which include the schools and universities maintained with state resources, as well as all the private intermediate and secondary schools within each state territory); and the municipal systems (which include public and private preschools and primary schools). As with the rest of its federative system, the Brazilian judiciary operates at both the federal and state levels.

According to the NEA, the schooling levels are structured as follows: basic education, with four levels: daycare (birth to three), preschool (ages three to five), fundamental education (ages six to fourteen), and secondary education (ages fifteen to seventeen); higher education, with two levels: undergraduate and graduate courses. Higher education should become equally accessible to all based on students' individual ability, through all suitable means, and especially as a result of the progressive implementation of free lower education.

In terms of public education,[1] the Brazilian educational system is different across states and municipalities in addition to being different from the educational systems at the federal level and in the Federal District. Federal entities are entitled to legislate about their own education systems as long as they abide by the Federal Constitution, the NEL, the NEP, and the ECA guidelines.

As a result, education systems, both in private and public schools, are free to decide how to provide education in response to local needs and about the right services for each community, including the power to create general rules of conduct, which may be supplemented by each educational institution individually, pursuant to the NEL.

The rationale of this model is decentralization through the allocation of specific incumbencies to each level of government, local, state, and federal, all of which have to comply with mandatory minimum revenue investments established by the constitution. Municipal governments are mainly responsible for preschool and fundamental education; state governments are mainly responsible for secondary education, which includes, as mentioned before, technical and vocational schools; the federal government is obliged to supplement the local and regional education budget, thus guaranteeing equal opportunities of access to education.

To support the previously mentioned educational commitments, the resources are guaranteed by a binding share of the tax revenue, pursuant to Article 212 of the Constitution. According to Article 212, the federal government shall apply to education no less than 18 percent, and the states, the Federal District, and the municipalities, at least 25 percent of the tax revenues annually.[2] These percentages are mandatory and when not applied accordingly, federal government intervention in the states, and likewise the state intervention in municipalities, is allowed by the constitution.

Since 1996, all three government levels in Brazil are obliged to allocate 60 percent of the previously mentioned resources in the universalization of fundamental education and better salaries for teachers.[3] In December 2006, this obligation was extended to basic education (fundamental and secondary).[4] To implement this, two temporary funds were created: the Fund for the Maintenance and Development of Fundamental Education (FUNDEF) and the Fund for the Maintenance and Development of Basic Education (FUNDEB).

The financial mechanism used in FUNDEF, and maintained by FUNDEB, is as follows: the resources of the fund are collected from federal, state, and municipal taxes and fiscal contributions, and redistributed according to the number of students enrolled annually in the public schools maintained by each governmental entity, based on a minimum value per student established by the federal government. The federal government has the duty to supplement the fund whenever, in each state and in the Federal District, the nationally set minimum amount per student is nor reached by the respective government entity.

The distribution of the resources will also prioritize enrollments from the first to the eighth grades of fundamental schooling. The rationale behind establishing a single educational fund, such as FUNDEF and then FUNDEB, was to rationalize the allocation of public educational resources, as well as to distribute the responsibilities and resources among the states and the municipalities.

The new education fund, FUNDEB, is expected to last fourteen years, when the target of 47.2 million students enrolled in basic education is achieved. The existing funds do not disoblige the states, the Federal District, and the municipalities from applying the remaining 40 percent of the statutory share of their taxes education.

From everything that has been noted, it can be stated that the right to education in Brazil is a *sui generis* overarching right, or a full-fledged fundamental right. Under these constitutional provisions, Article 227 provides the full protection of the child and adolescent. It is from this viewpoint that the topic of restorative justice and mediation in school violence matters—thus, including criminal violence as well as any form of verbal abuse, such as bullying and intimidation, or the breaking of school rules—and presents itself as a legally possible alternative and, above all, a desirable one.

The Full Protection of Children and Adolescents under the Brazilian Constitution

The Brazilian Constitution establishes full and equal protection for children and adolescents. This is a sort of affirmative policy whose origin is the acknowledgment by the legal system that the character of children and adolescents is different from that of adults, thereby requiring special legal provisions and specific protection due to their potentially vulnerable nature. The concept of potential vulnerability refers to the faint possibility children and adolescents have of enjoying, enforcing, or protecting their rights since they are human beings in formation.

The full protection of the child and adolescent was originally set out in the 1959 Declaration of the Rights of the Child. Its principles were later included as specific obligations of the signatory states of the United Nations

Convention on the Rights of the Child, the CRC, adopted by the General Assembly of the United Nations on November 20, 1989, and ratified by Brazil on November 24, 1990.

For the purposes of the CRC, as set in Article 1, "a child means every human being below the age of eighteen years unless under the law applicable to the child, majority is attained earlier." In regard to the right to education and student misconduct, Article 28.2 of the CRC declares that "State Parties shall take all appropriate measures to ensure that school discipline is administered in a manner consistent with the child's human dignity and in conformity with the present Convention."

Under the Brazilian Constitution, full protection is manifested through a set of rights and guarantees under Article 227, supplemented by Articles 226, 228e, 229, and also through the Child and Adolescent Act. This set of norms determines major priority in protecting and fostering the rights of children and adolescents.

Full protection also touches other dimensions of the life of children and adolescents as established under paragraph 3 of Article 227, among which are a minimum age of fourteen years for admission to work; a guarantee of social security and labor rights; a guarantee of access to school for the adolescent worker; due process of law and due process hearings in accordance with the specific legislation of the child and adolescent protection and in compliance with the principles of brevity, when applying any measures that restrain freedom; government social and medical assistance, including prevention and specialized assistance programs for children and adolescents addicted to narcotics or related drugs.

At the same time, adolescents under eighteen years of age may not be held criminally liable and shall be subject to the rules of the special legislation (Article 228). This understanding is supported by the principle of the child's absolute priority stated in Article 3.1. of the CRC: "In all actions concerning children, whether undertaken by public or private social welfare institutions, courts of law, administrative authorities or legislative bodies, the best interests of the child shall be a primary consideration."[5]

One of the greatest difficulties in incorporating international treaties to national laws is the translation of the wording of the original. However, even when translation is not an issue per se, in the case of the CRC, for instance, the phrase "the best interests of the child" [*o interesse maior da criança*] has received a wider interpretation in Brazil due to Article 227 of the constitution.

The Superior Federal Courts, in a series of cases, ruled that reductions invoking protection of children and adolescents, especially in cases concerning criminal acts, should give the widest efficacy to the norms applicable to those who the constitution aimed to protect most.[6]

As a result of this interpretation, state (the *Tribunais de Justiça*) and federal courts, including the Brazilian Supreme Court (*Supremo Tribunal Federal* [STF]) and the Brazilian Superior Court of Justice (*Superior Tribunal de Justiça* [STJ]), for instance, have fined negligent or lenient parents who overlook the school evasion of their children[7] despite the fact that the negligence of parents when it comes to the welfare of their children is a crime according to Article 249 of the ECA.

Along the same line of thought, cases seeking the recovery of tuition from students who are enrolled in private schools have been decided in favor of the students. Brazilian courts have agreed that school officials cannot deny students enrollment or consider their agreement terminated during, but only at the end of, school years.[8]

The views here are mirrored when applying the ECA and it is under their perspective that issues concerning student misconduct should be examined, notably the adoption of codes of behavior, the duty of care, violence prevention as responsibility of the school, and the responsibility for the failure to prevent bullying and potential liability on part of the school; legal powers of search and confiscation; the power to use "reasonable force" as a restraining measure; antisocial behavior; liability in case of violence, among others. These issues are addressed next in general terms in the light of the ECA.

THE ECA AND STUDENT MISCONDUCT

Brazil has no specific laws on student misconduct and violence in schools. Even so, the ECA plays an essential role in defining the responsibilities of family members and guardians as well as of school and government authorities based on the full protection doctrine set out in the Federal Constitution (Article 227), which focuses on protecting young people aged twelve to eighteen from all forms of negligence, discrimination, exploitation, abuse, cruelty, and oppression.

The ECA's top priority in terms of basic education, then, is to have children and youngsters come first when government policies, use of government money, and the actions of governors, lawmakers, families, the community, and society are concerned. It also means that those rights must be sufficiently protected by families, society, and the government, who all share responsibility for ensuring them. Article 98 of the ECA provides a broad array of protective measures. Among the most significant measures in the ECA are medical, psychological, and psychiatric care as well as government assistance programs for families, children, and adolescents (Article 101).

In light of such principles, the ECA contains provisions granting the right to education, culture, sport, and leisure. Article 53 of the act ensures, among other things, the right of youngsters to be respected by their teachers and to question grading methods, individually or through their representatives, and to bring the case to higher educational authorities or even to the courts.

The ECA is less specific, though, in terms of defining the duties children and adolescents have in regard to their schools, peers, and teachers. Nor is the ECA more specific concerning the duties of the school in regard to their students. Even so, the courts have created case law to account for this lack of specific provisions since, as has been noticed in the bullying cases, in which jurists have found there is strict liability on the part of school systems with regard to victims, when there is evidence that officials were negligent or ineffective in taking the necessary measures to solve the problems.[9]

Under the ECA, only crimes and misdemeanors are considered offenses (Article 103). Nevertheless, under Brazilian law, since people under the age of eighteen lack legal capacity, they cannot be charged with crimes. If those under eighteen commit wrongs, they are subject to socio-educational measures set out in Article 116 including the duty to repair the damages caused, perform community service, and supervised freedom subject to due process.

In this context, socio-educational detention measures are exceptions and can only be established by the courts under Article 122 (wrong committed through threats or violence to the person; repeat of serious offenses; or systematically or unreasonably not complying with socio-educational measures). Detention restrictions are subject to the principle of shortness of detention periods and respect to adolescents' conditions of not yet fully developed persons.

Based on the preceding paragraph, the Brazilian Supreme Court is establishing case law in the light of the fact that adolescents are entitled to positive protection measures, including restorative justice, and in the light of the *sui generis* norms ensured by the constitution (Articles 227 and 228), detention measures shall not be established solely based on the seriousness of the act committed by the adolescent.[10]

Government policies designed to deter inappropriate behavior and abuse in the state of São Paulo's public schools view the ECA as being protective rather than punitive provisions. In fact, the ECA implicitly entails and recommends the restorative model under a variety of provisions, especially when providing for remission (Article 126) and in view of the wide scope of socio-educational measures under Article 112ff.

Accordingly, to avoid criminalizing and judicializing interpersonal relations characterized by inappropriate behavior and abuse at school under the ECA, such policies encourage the representatives of all school segments to create rules clearly establishing the rights and duties of each member of school communities and to identify which measures should be taken by educators in case the previously established and mutually agreed to rules are broken.

Victim support and healing is thus a priority; offenders take responsibility for what they have done and look at how to avoid future offending; dialogue is a tool to achieve understanding and, as a result, the community helps to reintegrate both victims and offenders. Such measures meet the recommendations of the ECOSOC Resolution 2002/12, adopted on July 24, 2002, by the member-states of the United Nations, drawing out the basic principles on the use of restorative justice to solve conflicts resulting from school misconduct.

According to Resolution 2002/12, "restorative justice programme" means a program using restorative processes and seeks to achieve restorative outcomes. Restorative processes, in turn, mean

> any process in which the victim and the offender, and, where appropriate, any other individual or community member affected by a crime, participate in arising from the crime, generally with the help of a facilitator.
> Restorative processes may include mediation, conciliation, conferencing, and sentencing circles.

In this context, mediation is a process in which an impartial third party helps to deter students' inappropriate behavior and abuse, aiming at bringing the parties to understandings and, if necessary, repairing the injuries.

In the state of São Paulo, restorative justice is employed in juvenile courts and in special courts located in the state capital that is carried out in partnership with the Department of Education. From the perspective of the courts, research conducted by Adriana Silveira (2010) showed that from when the ECA was enacted in 1991 until 2008, only a small number of suits concerning the right to education were filed with the court of appeals of the state of São Paulo.

Regarding the cases of expulsion and suspension, the courts limited their analysis to whether due process of law was satisfied and individual rights ensured. In other words, courts granted school officials broad discretion to ensure safe and orderly learning environments insofar as school boards have the authority to adopt reasonable policies and procedures regulating student conduct.

These developments represent a giant step forward when one takes into account that prior to the enactment of the ECA, the statutory provisions on juvenile delinquency stemmed from the former Juvenile Code (Law 6697/79) which was blatantly discriminatory in content, considering children and adolescents not as holders of rights but rather as individuals lacking capacity but subject to repressive measures.

Drafted during the Brazilian military dictatorship and in line with the spirit of the time, the Juvenile Code consolidated the "abnormal situation doctrine," which stigmatized children and adolescents who experienced addiction problems or were otherwise affected by exclusion, family distress, economic and social hardships.

Another critical step forward taken by the ECA is the political and administrative decentralization enabling communities to control and oversee public policies aimed at children and adolescents through city councils (*Conselhos Municipais de Direitos*) and child protection councils (*Conselhos Tutelares*) (Article 131), the latter made up solely of citizens. This is a practice which allows continuous development of restorative justice programs as required by the ECOSOC Resolution 2002/12 in addition to creating and promoting a culture favorable to the use of restorative justice among law enforcement, judicial, and social authorities, as well as across schools and local communities.

THE STATE OF SÃO PAULO SCHOOL PROTECTION SYSTEM

The state of São Paulo is the most populated state in Brazil with approximately forty-one million residents distributed across 645 cities. Immigrants comprise approximately three million of the population. According to official data, in the state educational system, there is a rough average of 4.5 million students enrolled in more than five thousand public basic and secondary schools where two hundred thousand teachers are working under the oversight of the Department of Education. In 2010, this massive system was supported with a budget of almost twelve billion BRL (approximately six billion US dollars).[11]

The scenario of basic education in public schools of the state of São Paulo does not reflect the reality in other parts of the country. Even so, the situation in the state of São Paulo nonetheless can be used as reference for the general conditions of basic education found in public schools nationwide: the state of São Paulo has a huge school network that experiences social and educational problems arising from the "universalization" of basic education, a system where the same social and economic problems surrounding the schools and the communities students come from are mirrored in the classroom.

There are also other relevant data to consider. Most teachers are not prepared to deal with the heterogeneity and diversity of their students in a violent environment. This lack of preparation can often be attributed to flaws in their initial teacher training. Under such circumstances, students and teachers being constantly late to, or absent from, school because there is little commitment from either side, and who both experience a feeling of not belonging to the school. This results in adverse effects to the quality of education.

There is no reliable official data on school violence resulting from student misconduct. This is because in most cases of violence the people involved, namely principals, teachers, and students, do not formally report their complaints or record them in the school books specifically kept for this purpose. The reason for this situation is because principals, teachers, and students experience, founded or unfounded, a fear of retaliation by the individuals or groups involved.

Research aimed at understanding violence in schools such as the work carried out by Ruotti, Alves, and Cubas (2006) and even by the Department of Education itself in an effort to adopt preventive and repressive measures are more based on the news and media than on police reports or school records. The problem lies not only in that the information broadcasted is not enough to assess the number of violent events in schools, but also in the fact that the press tends to give a generalized idea that public schools, especially those located in the outskirts of metropolitan regions such as the cities of São Paulo, Campinas and Santos are violent (Ruotti, Alves, and Cubas, 2006).

Since 2009 the School Reporting Register (*Registro de Ocorrências Escolares* [ROE]) has been introduced in the public state network. The ROE is an online system in which discipline or criminal issues in school environments are registered. The ROE is available to all principals of the state education network. The ROE's main objective is to record and map safety and discipline issues which can affect schools. Further, the ROE's aim is to build a dynamic database enabling the daily life of schools to be visualized to ensure the protection of the school environment, students, teachers, and employees.

The main challenge of the ROE is to permit users to gain understandings concerning the treatment given to the information gathered; this has been the cause of distorted views about ROE. Many principals do not use ROE because they believe the reports will not benefit their schools in any way. Others believe they will be punished because of how they dealt with situations.

On the other hand, there are principals who believe that inputting data in the ROE system will entitle them to extra pay due under the "working place premium" (*Adicional de Local de Exercício* [ALE]), which is an amount paid for state employees that work in high-vulnerability rate areas. Therefore, the lack of information on the use and goals of the ROE system results in its poor use and lack of reliability.

Another source of data on principals' perception of violence in schools is the questionnaire applied together with the education system's student's assessment, the so-called Saresp. The data in this questionnaire are used by the Secretariat of Education in assessing all of its other programs in place such as School of the Family (*Escola da Família*), Teaching Prevention (*Prevenção Também Se Ensina*), and Community inside the School (*Comunidade Presente*). The questionnaire assesses the perceptions of principals concerning the three groups of events below which are considered violence in schools

Table 1.1 SARESP Questionnaire Data

SARESP questionnaire data in relative numbers	SARESP 2008	SARESP 2010	SARESP 2008/ 2010
Theft, damage to property, and graffiti	59	53	−6
Violence against students, teachers or employees	47	48	−1
Fighting among students	89	85	−4
Average	65	62	−3

Source: São Paulo State Department of Education SARESP—Secretaria da Educação do Estado de São Paulo. Coordenadoria de informação, monitoramento e avaliação escolar. Desempenho escolar. Estado de São Paulo 2010/2012. http://www.educacao.sp.gov.br/a2sitebox/arquivos/documentos/433.pdf

(see table 1.1). From table 1.1 it is noticeable that between the questionnaire applied in 2008 and the one applied in 2010, there was a slight drop in violence rates (3 percent on average). According to research conducted by Ruotti in the east side of the city of São Paulo (districts of *Cidade Tiradentes*, *Iguatemi*, *São Mateus*, and *São Rafael*) and south side (districts of *Jardim Ângela*, *Jardim São Luis*, *Capão Redondo*, and *Campo Limpo*) of the city of São Paulo, inappropriate behavior is widespread. The various forms of inappropriate behavior or abuse in the daily life of basic education public schools ranges from "micro violence" such as name calling, rude words, pushing, and humiliating, which principals consider inappropriate behavior, to abuses regulated by the Criminal Code such as bombs damaging school property, larceny, threat, drug use and trafficking, and gun possession by students.

The research points to the fact that although some problems are linked to the specific features of the reality of each school, there are some general patterns of inappropriate behavior and abuse. Given the severity and frequency of how events vary considerably across schools, though, one cannot simply say that schools are always subject to the violence that surrounds the districts where they are located.

Another initiative, also in 2009, was the implementation of the School Protection System to articulate a set of actions, methods, and tools designed to disseminate best practices aimed at preventing conflicts in schools, integrating schools to the networks that ensure the rights of children and adolescents while promote the necessary forms of protection of school communities and public assets.

The fundamental idea is to change the informal rules of conduct, which are likely to foster violence in schools. The system's main focus is on aggres-

..anging school social cultures and patterns of interaction among ..ent groups of students, teachers, and teacher assistants with different backgrounds.

The legal framework under which the system operates was established under the "General Rules of Conduct for State Public Schools" issued by the Department of Education in 2009. These rules were developed in light of the previously mentioned constitutional principles on the right to education and the full protection of children and adolescents, which are part of the Basic Internal Rules for State Public Schools of 1998. These rules of conduct have the nature of general guidelines which are not enforceable in the sense that they do not consist of codes of conduct that attach immediately applicable penalties to certain types of conduct.

The purpose of such rules is to help school leaders define their own rules of behavior set out in the *School Protection and Citizenship Handbook*, with sections devoted to how to live together and face any weaknesses that schools may have. The handbook is designed to address situations about which educational professionals long complained such as rights and duties, responsibilities, and restrictions at schools, student punishment, lack of autonomy, and authority for the principal to act independently in the event of violations as well as the expected behavior of students in classroom and even inside or outside the school building.[12]

The General Rules of Conduct for State Public Schools (GRC) (Annex I) aim to ensure socially accepted rules of conduct based on policies and procedures that satisfy due process. These rules describe student rights, duties, and responsibilities along with misbehavior subject to disciplinary measures. In addition, under the GRC, conduct that teachers or the school officials deem inappropriate for healthy school or learning and teaching environments are subject to disciplinary penalties.

Student infractions described in note 4 of the GRC include a wide variety of forms of misconduct.[13] The penalties that school officials can impose on students vary from verbal warnings to suspensions, expulsions, or mandatory transfers to other schools as set out in number 6 of the GRC. Additional disciplinary measures may be applied involving parents and guardians in school activities, providing individual or group counseling to mediate conflict situations and holding counseling meetings for parents or guardians.

The persons responsible for acting in these cases are School and Community Mediator-Teachers (SCMTs). These professionals have been trained through continuing education courses. Among the duties of the SCMT are adopting mediation and restorative justice practices in potential conflicts within school environments, interviewing parents or guardians, analyzing situations of vulnerability to which students may be exposed, assisting the family or guardians in seeking the help of social workers, and so on. The main purpose of SCMTs is to accompany students' interaction with the other members of school communities and to develop an educational plan to enhance the protection of school communities, avoiding situations of vulnerability and conflicts inherent to such interactions.

In addition to the mediator-teacher programs, two other programs are operative. The first, Prevention Can Be Taught, is aimed at reducing students' vulnerability in relation to the use of alcohol, tobacco, and other drugs along with preventing teenage pregnancy. The second, Community Present, encourages discussion of subjects relating to human rights, ethics, and citizenship while proposing communication actions seeking to promote nonviolence and peaceful resolution of conflicts.

Moreover, with the support of the State Department of Public Safety, state schools have been hosting talks on the fight against drug use. Designed for children and adolescents, the Drug and Abuse Resistance Education Program (PROERD) is conducted by police officers and the main purpose of such initiative is to help students understand the hazards caused by drugs. Since their implementation, school violence prevention programs have been supplementing other well-established programs and projects within the state school network that deal with the subject of school interaction from different standpoints. The Family School Program and the Prevention Can Be Taught program are part of this set of programs. The latter is a program that offers support to the school team by handing out educational material and by holding workshops that qualify school professionals to skillfully deal with topics such as sexually transmitted diseases, AIDS, sexuality, diversity, drug use, and bullying.

At the same time, the State Department of Education has been promoting continuing education courses designed for all teachers and employees of the public state school network. These courses involve specific knowledge on full protection of children and adolescents, peaceful resolution of conflicts, and the duties of each and every individual that is part of the network that was designed to ensure the rights of children and adolescents.

SCHOOL AND COMMUNITY MEDIATOR-TEACHERS

The creation of roles for SCMTs is a new concept in the public schools since 2010. In the administrative law perspective, this is an important hallmark in the public teachers' career. In fact, as a constitutional general rule, careers, salaries, professional statutes, and benefits are established by law. As a result, public school teachers are only admitted through qualifying examinations, a rule stipulated by all former constitutions, with no exceptions, which entitle them to tenured positions after three years of teaching.

The accumulation of public positions is forbidden by the constitution as a general rule (Article 37, XVI). Even so, teachers in the public system are allowed to be remunerated for two teaching positions or one teaching position together with another technical or scientific job as long as there is a compatibility of working hours between the two sets of professional duties. As such, being a SCMT implies, at least, a personal renouncement of accumulated teaching positions.

Another turning point in the SCMT program is the use of pedagogical approaches to deal with micro violence situations excluding punitive approaches that are still believed to be necessary in schools. These approaches include, among other measures, alternative methods of conflict resolution such as mediation and restorative justice that are widespread in the law field. In school environments, the main axes of conflict resolution are understanding that conflicts are natural; understanding that conflicts are educational opportunities; understanding the need to hold accountable those involved in conflicts; anticipating the full consequences of individuals' actions and restoring the harm done to someone.

This approach greatly differs from simple punishment without accountability and without repairing the harm caused. It also spreads a culture based on consensus of the people involved. In this scenario, training teachers to act as SCMTs is an important step which includes, besides the pedagogical content, concepts and methodologies to alternative dispute resolutions, as well as preparing the teacher to better understand the rights of children and adolescents. Likewise, introducing and implementing the SCMT programs in schools is crucial for their success and has been gradually carried out through the schools' voluntary adherence.

To assess the function of SCMT, the Department of Education, in 2011, applied a lengthy questionnaire, which was sent out to 830 school principals, deputy principals, and coordinating teachers of the public schools of all Regional Education Offices.[14] From the answers provided, it is possible to state that the program is well-accepted among the school communities surveyed. What is more, there is an inflection in the curves regarding the record of conflicts in the school environment. Before, there was an upward trend in conflicts. After the implementation of the programs, the trend has been downward.

Regarding the acceptance of the SCMT program, 25 percent of respondents indicated that it exceeded their expectations, 46 percent thought that it met their expectations, and 17 percent noted it is still too early to assess its impact. When asked whether they wish mediators to continue working, 90 percent answered yes. As a whole, 88 percent of respondents viewed the contribution of the program in improving the school environment as good or very good, compared to 5 percent who said it was poor or very poor. As to teaching and learning conditions, 76 percent responded the contribution of the program was good or very good, while 9 percent considered it to be poor or very poor. As to improving student performance in school, 75 percent of respondents indicated that the PMEC's contribution was good or very good against 9 percent who said it was poor or very poor.

Creating the role of SCMTs to act in the state school network has contributed to disseminating nonpunitive methods of conflict resolution, to shaping and bringing together the means that ensure the rights involved at a given school area, to following up—on a systematic, non-isolated basis—on conflicts in the school environment. Three years after the creation of the SCMT, 2,447 teachers have played the role of mediator-teachers in 2,116 of the 5,200 state public schools. Since then, 3,133 mediator-teachers have been trained. Further, child and youth care workers are trained by the Department of Education to mediate school violence.

Regardless of the highly positive assessment results of the School Protection Systems, a means of bringing peace to schools, its efforts must still be improved and increased. A review of the internal rules of state public schools is an example. Such rules must outline the escalation procedure in relation to inappropriate behavior and less offensive actions. These procedures must be agreed on by the entities comprising the networks designed to ensure the rights of children and adolescents as they offer social protection, to student bodies and faculty, parents, and relatives. Training on alternative dispute resolution methods, such as mediation and restorative circles, must be given within the scope of the SCMT program. In addition, local child and adolescent protection committees must be assisted through the participation of community institutions and social workers.

CONCLUSION

Brazil has no specific laws on student misconduct and violence in schools. Even so, the ECA plays an essential role in defining the responsibilities of family members and guardians as well as of school and government authorities based on the full protection doctrine set out in the Federal Constitution (Article 227), which focuses on protecting young people aged twelve to eighteen from all forms of negligence, discrimination, exploitation, abuse, cruelty, and oppression.

Based on the preceding, the Brazilian Supreme Court is developing case law in the light of the fact that adolescents are entitled to positive protection measures, including restorative justice. In the state of São Paulo, restorative justice is employed in juvenile courts and in special courts located in the state capital that is carried out in partnership with the Department of Education.

In addition, the Department of Education created the School Protection System to consolidate a set of actions and methods aimed at preventing conflicts in school environments. In this sense, school protection refers to a broad set of factors influencing the process of teaching and learning such as safety, living in tolerant environments and social inclusion of all members of the communities where schools are located. The system's main features are its systemic character, involving the community, since a school cannot act alone against social phenomena as complex as violence, insecurity, or conflict.

The persons responsible for acting in the system are the SCMTs, whose duties included adopting mediation and restorative justice practices in potential conflicts within school environments, interviewing parents or guardians, analyzing situations of vulnerability to which students may be exposed, assisting the family or guardians in seeking the help of social workers, and so on.

In schools, the use of restorative practices has proven to be a reliable tool to reduce misbehavior, bullying, violence, and crime among students and improve overall learning environments in Brazil. Nonetheless, as recommended by the UN ECOSOC Resolution 2002/12, the São Paulo State Department of Education should continue to promote research and evaluation of the School Protection Systems to assess the extent to which they result in restorative outcomes while serving as a supplement or alternative to the criminal justice system, providing positive outcomes for all parties. Adopting such an approach could lead to a legislative reform in the organizations of schools and the careers of teachers, which would be an important advance considering the size of the public education system and its corporative environment.

Key Points

1. Although Brazil has no specific laws on student misconduct and violence in schools, the ECA plays an essential role in defining the responsibilities of family members and guardians along with school officials.
2. Officials in Brazilian schools have effectively used restorative practices to reduce student misbehavior, bullying, violence, and crime.
3. Through active interventions, educational leaders in São Paulo have helped to make schools safer learning environments for all.

NOTES

1. In Brazil, the term "public schools" refers to those which are free of charge and are maintained by local or state governments.

2. Education and health are the only public social areas which are objects of statutory funding in the form of a share of the revenue from taxes (Articles 167, IV and 218, paragraph 5). Article 167, of the Federal Constitution clearly makes an exception to the general rule against attaching tax revenues to a certain public agency, fund, or expense. Article 218 also

provides that the states and the Federal District may allocate a share of their budgetary revenues to public entities which foster scientific and technological education and research.

3. Amendment 14, September 12, 1996.

4. Amendment 53, December 20, 2006.

5. The origins of the *best interest of the child* principle date as far back as English feudalism and the need to protect the vulnerable from the crown. It entered American law in the twentieth century and was recognized by the Supreme Court in *Finlay v. Finlay* (1925; 240 N.Y. 429), with Justice Cardozo's winning opinion. In *Finlay*, after their divorce, the parents were battling for the custody of their children through mutual accusations of irresponsibility. The court took into account the "best interests of the child," regardless of looking into the responsibility of either mother or father. See also *Yale Law Journal*, December 1925, Case note *235 Equity-Powers under the Doctrine of Parens Patriae (1925) by the Yale Law Journal Company, Inc., Westlaw documents, 170902.

6. STF, Appel in Writ of Mandamus 108.970/DF; STJ, Appel in Writ of Mandamus 33.620—MG). See also http://redir.stf.jus.br/paginadorpub/paginador.jsp?docTP=TP&docID=1641450; https://ww2.stj.jus.br/revistaeletronica/Abre_Documento.asp?sLink=ATC&sSeq=19423383&sReg=201100128232&sData=20111219&sTipo=5&formato=PDF.

7. As seen in the decision of the Civil Appeal 1.0687.07.054286-9/0001 *Tribunal de Justiça de Minas Gerais*; and in the Civil Appeal 0004894-37.2004.8.19.0046 *Tribunal de Justiça do Rio de Janeiro*, among others.

8. See (*Tribunal de Justiça do Distrito Federal* 2007.0020.020.331).

9. See *Tribunal de Justiça do Distrito Federal*, Civil Appeal 20060310083312-DF.

10. Habeas Corpus 114 914/SP; HC 105 91/PE.

11. Secretaria da Educação do Estado de São Paulo. Censo Escolar de 2011, http://www.educacao.sp.gov.br/a2sitebox/arquivos/documentos/547.pdf.

12. The School Protection and Citizenship Handbook was adapted from the School Managers Handbook from the State Department of Education of the Federal District; the General Rules of Conduct for State Public Schools were inspired in the Discipline Code of the City of New York.

13. Among the misbehaviors identified are disrespecting, disregarding, or insulting school administrators, teachers, or employees; arriving at schools under the effect of substances that are harmful to the student's health or to social interaction; exhibiting or distributing defamatory, racist or biased texts, literature or material, including exhibiting said material on the internet; engaging in illegal activities during school hours such as buying, stealing, transporting, or distributing forthcoming examinations or their correct answers, in whole or in part; damaging or destroying school equipment, material, or facilities; writing on, scrawling on, or marking up school walls, windows, doors, or sports courts; threatening the school with a bomb threat; making comments or insinuations with an aggressive or disrespectful sexual connotation or engaging in any sexually offensive behavior; encouraging or participating in acts of vandalism that intentionally damage school equipment, materials, and facilities or the belongings of any member of the school community or others; consuming, carrying, distributing, or selling controlled substances, and alcohol or other legal or illegal drugs on school grounds.

14. SPEC, Secretaria da Educação do Estado de São Paulo. Sistema de proteção escolar. http://www.educacao.sp.gov.br/spec/.

REFERENCES

Declaration of the Rights of the Child. (1959). http://www.un.org/cyberschoolbus/humanrights/resources/child.asp.

De Groof, J., and G. Lauwers. (2006). *The Right to Education and Rights in Education.* Nijmegen: Wolf Legal Publishers.

Machado, Martha de Toledo. (2003). A proteção constitucional de crianças e adolescentes e os direitos humanos. São Paulo: Manole.

———, Direito da Infancia e da Juventude. (2009). In Nunes Jr., Vidal Serrano (cord.), Manual de Direitos Difusos, São Paulo: Ed. Verbatim.

São Paulo State Department of Education (Secretaria de Estado da Educação de São Paulo). (2011). General Rules of Conduct for State Public Schools, Office of Assessment and School Performance Index (Gerência de Avaliação e Indicadores de Rendimento Escolar) of the Educational Development Foundation (Fundação para o Desenvolvimento da Educação).

São Paulo State Department of Education (Secretaria de Estado da Educação de São Paulo) (2011). School Protection and Citizenship Supervisory Office (Supervisão de Proteção Escolar e Cidadania).

Ruotti, C., A. Renato, and V. Cubas de Oliveira. (2006). In Violência na Escola: Um Guia para Pais e Professores [Violence at School: a Guide for Parents and Teachers], São Paulo, 1st edition, Imprensa Oficial, 259 pages.

Silveira, A. D. (2010). O Direito à Educação de Crianças e Adolescentes: análise da atuação do Tribunal de Justiça de São Paulo (1991–2008) [Children's and Adolescents' Right to Education: An Analysis of the Decisions Rendered by the São Paulo Court of Appeals (1991–2008)] Doctoral Thesis, School of Education of the University of São Paulo (Faculdade de Educação da Universidade de São Paulo).

United Nations. (2002). ECOSOC Resolution 2002/12, Basic principles on the use of restorative justice programmes in criminal matters.

Chapter Two

Student Discipline in China[1]

Suping Shen, Jun Wang, and Ran Zhang

This chapter introduces practices for student misconduct and the related laws in China. Two aspects of these topics are of particular interest. First, China traditionally is a Confucian society. In Confucian tradition, the "appropriate order" of the teacher-student relationship is prescribed in such a way as students are to respect their teachers and follow their commands. Second, beginning in the late 1970s, China launched economic and legal reforms as officials sought to establish a system of "rule of law." In this process, educational statutes have been enacted and various ministry and local rules have been passed to govern education. Despite being immature and incomplete, the legal regulations for student discipline have gained their initial shape but have kept evolving.

The chapter begins with a brief introduction of the Chinese legal system. This short overview outlines the sources of law and a few legal principles important in understanding practices for student misconduct in China. Immediately following this look at the legal landscape, the chapter sketches a picture of the prevalence, forms, and patterns of student misconduct by drawing on empirical studies. Then the chapter examines, in detail, the methods of student discipline and due process measures available. This section also highlights special considerations in student discipline in China. The chapter concludes with a summary and discussion of future directions of student discipline in China.

INTRODUCTION TO THE LEGAL SYSTEM

The major sources of education law in China consist primarily of a hierarchical system of legal codes, including the Constitution, statutes, State Council regulations, provincial and local legislation, ministry regulations, legislation, and rules in the self-governing ethnic minority regions, and international covenants or conventions. Among these sources of law, the most relevant to student misconduct are the educational statutes, Ministry of Education regulations, and regulations issued by provincial or local educational agencies.

School rules are not recognized as official sources of law in China but are usually respected unless they conflict with upper-level laws. While the rest of the chapter is devoted to specific educational and legal details concerning student misconduct, this section explains key legal principles necessary to understand how educators deal with student misconduct in China.

Elementary and secondary education is directly managed by local governments in China; however, the central government still plays a crucial leadership role.[2] In China, education is defined in the Constitution of 1982 as a fundamental right of citizens.[3]

Different from a federal system of government, the central government in China has the power to regulate educational practices throughout the entire nation. As a result, school officials and teachers must observe national statutes and Ministry of Education regulations before all other rules and regulations on the subject. Among these statutes, the Education Law (1995), Teacher Law (1993), Compulsory Education Law (2006), and Law on Protection of Minors (2006) each contain provisions pertaining to student discipline.

China has a nine-year compulsory schooling system which covers elementary and junior secondary education.[4] This compulsory system contains two important components. First, once children reach the age of six (as a general rule) or seven (in poor areas), their parents are legally obligated to send their children to school.[5]

Second, compulsory education is free such that parents do not have to pay tuition or fees for their children to attend elementary or junior secondary school.[6] Given this compulsory nature of schooling, students in elementary and junior secondary school are immune from certain types of disciplinary measures that would remove them from school attendance.

Insofar as most elementary and secondary school students fall below the age of majority (eighteen years old)[7] in China, their parents or other legal guardians[8] are often involved in the student discipline process. If the misconduct of minors causes damage to other persons, then their guardians shall assume the tort liability.[9] If minors have property under their name, then the damages shall be first paid out of their property with the guardian only being responsible for any remaining deficit.[10]

STUDENT MISCONDUCT IN SCHOOL AND ITS FORMS

Student misconduct is a problem in Chinese schools, but to a lesser degree than occurs in some Western countries.[11] In one survey of 527 teachers from twenty-seven elementary schools located in five provinces, about 45 percent of the teachers reported spending "too much time" on student behavior problems.[12] Among the 244 elementary and secondary school teachers surveyed in another study, 56 percent did not regard classroom management as a great concern.[13]

The most frequent and troublesome form of student classroom misbehavior as perceived by Chinese teachers is nonattention.[14] Other major behavioral problems include disruptive behaviors during class, skipping class or school, teasing, profanity and swearing, vandalism, disobedience, smoking, drinking, intimidation or harassment of other students, fighting, cheating on tests, and theft.[15]

The prevalence of student misconduct differs by gender and location. For example, boys have consistently been found to have more behavioral problems than girls.[16] Rural schools often have a higher rate of student misconduct than urban schools.[17] This regional disparity is possibly related to the fact that rural areas are far less developed than urban locales and many children in rural settings must live apart from their parents who migrate to cities or coastal areas to earn a living.

The prevalence of specific forms of student misconduct may also vary by grade or level of school. While minor forms of behavior disorders are dominant in elementary school, physically aggressive and immoral behaviors become more prevalent in secondary schools.[18] Probably because of the intensive study pressure in the last year of junior secondary and senior secondary schools, the prevalence of fighting at that level drops slightly from the previous year. In comparison, the prevalence of cheating on tests increases by each grade, becoming a major reason for student discipline in secondary schools and colleges or universities.[19]

METHODS OF STUDENT DISCIPLINE

The methods of student discipline in China fall into two broad categories: formal sanctions by the school (*chufen*) authorities and informal discipline by the teachers (*chengjie*). Formal sanctions are made available by state laws and local rules. The formal sanctions are applicable to relatively severe forms of misconduct through a formal decision-making process at the school level. In contrast, the informal discipline methods are used by teachers in their classroom management on a daily basis. Except for the clear ban on corporal punishment, the laws have been largely silent on the legal status of those informal discipline methods.

Formal Methods: Sanctions Rendered by Schools

The Education Law (1995) affords school authorities the power to impose sanctions on misbehaving students[20] but does not directly specify what types of sanctions are available. Various Ministry of Education regulations and provincial administrative rules include the following formal methods of student discipline (*chufen*): warning (*jinggao*), severe warning (*yanzhong jinggao*), documentation of violation (*jiguo*), probation (*liuxiao chakan*), involuntary withdrawal from school (*leling tuixue*), and expulsion (*kaichu xueji*).[21]

Some or all of these disciplinary methods may be in effect in a particular school. The conditions for the application of each disciplinary method are usually specified at the school level. In most provinces, the warnings, severe warnings, documentations of violations, and probation methods are established at the school level; decisions on involuntary withdrawal and expulsion must be further approved by local education bureaus.[22]

Involuntary withdrawal from school and expulsion are reserved for the most outrageous forms of student misconduct and apply only to senior secondary school students. Students in the compulsory education stages, namely elementary and junior secondary schools, are excluded from their application.[23] As the most severe type of disciplinary action, expulsion results in a termination of a student's status at a particular school. Involuntary withdrawal is similar as, even though a student is not directly expelled, he is forced to withdraw from the school.

It should be noted that some localities impose more restrictions on the application of disciplinary sanctions than others. For example, within the Shanghai municipality regular formal methods of student discipline in the elementary and secondary schools only includes the warning, severe warning, documentation of violation, and probation methods. Expulsion is not included in this list of regular disciplinary sanctions and is applicable only to senior secondary school students who have committed a criminal offense. Further, while probation is usually directly rendered by local school officials, in Shanghai, educators need additional confirmation from their local educational bureaus.[24]

Informal Methods: Discipline by Teachers

The previously mentioned methods of student discipline are school actions and do not cover informal disciplinary measures used by teachers in classrooms. The laws in China are silent on the disciplining (*chengjie*) powers of teachers. In practice, Chinese teachers have used a wide variety of discipline methods including, but not limited to, verbal reprimands, time-outs, confiscations, and detentions. Chinese teachers sometimes also adapt an array of educational practices, such as requiring students to hand copy texts or calling teacher-parent conferences, into possible disciplinary measures.

While suspension is not available in Chinese schools as a formal method of student discipline, teachers sometimes use time-outs to remove a disruptive student temporarily from classrooms. In time-out sessions, students can be asked to stand in the back of classrooms, right outside of classrooms, or in the teachers' offices.

Chinese teachers also sometimes use physical labor or exercise as a method of student discipline. Teachers may order students who misbehaved or did not complete their homework to clean classrooms, run on playgrounds, or copy their homework by hand multiple times.

Interestingly, teacher-parent conferences have become another informal method of student discipline in Chinese schools. After students misbehave, teachers may ask their parents to come to the school for conferences. For many students, they would prefer hand copying texts a dozen times or spend a few hours in teachers' offices than invite their parents to school.[25] In other words, teacher-parent conferences are no longer just communication platform; they are threats that Chinese teachers use in student behavior management as a disciplinary method.

Chinese law does not explicitly afford teachers the power of student discipline but it does clearly outlaw corporal punishment as discipline. The Compulsory Education Law (2006),[26] Law on Protection of Minors (2006),[27] and Teacher Law (1993)[28] prohibit the application of corporal punishment on students. Teachers who use corporal punishment despite being warned not to do so may be subject to civil, administrative and, sometimes, even criminal liability.[29]

It must be noted that this prohibition also extends to "covert corporal punishment" (*bianxiang tifa*). However, the law fails to define this term. In practice, some of the informal disciplinary measures mentioned earlier, such as having students stand during class periods, engage in physical exercise, or hand copy texts, may be recognized as "covert" forms of corporal punishment (*bianxiang tifa*). Teachers who use those informal methods can be vulnerable to legal challenges.

Statistics show that Chinese teachers fairly often use these informal disciplinary methods. According to a large scale self-reported survey of elementary and junior secondary school students from ten provinces, 29 percent of students were detained after school for punishment, 12.1 percent were kept out of their classrooms during instructional time, 40.3 percent were ordered to stand during instruction time or run on playgrounds, 37.8 percent were required to hand copy texts or homework assignments multiple times, and

15.4 percent were subjected to corporal punishment from their teachers (despite its illegal status in Chinese schools).[30]

In comparison, formal methods of student discipline, which are rendered at the school level, were far less likely to be used. A survey of elementary, junior secondary, and senior secondary school students in two districts of Beijing showed that 95.7 percent of the students had not been subject to any disciplinary sanctions. Among the 4.3 percent who were sanctioned by their schools, 1.5 percent received a warning, 1.1 percent received a severe warning, 1.6 percent received a documentation of violation, and 0.1 percent received probation.[31]

DUE PROCESS

Due process is a relatively new idea in student discipline in China. In *Tian Yong v. Beijing University of Science and Technology* (1999), a trial court in Beijing ruled that university officials violated the student's rights to notice and defense in the face of a negative decision that they rendered.[32] This case was printed in the *Supreme People Court Gazette*, the official journal of the Supreme People Court, the highest level of the judiciary in China, and serves as precedent guiding the rulings in future similar cases. As one of the most important education law cases in China, the *Tian Yong* introduced the notion of due process to student affairs at educational institutions.

In 2005, the Ministry of Education issued the new *Regulation on Student Record Management in General Higher Education Institutions*, which required institutional officials to provide students undergoing disciplinary processes with a series of due process measures. Although the Ministry of Education regulations relevant to elementary or secondary school management have stayed intact, recently revised provincial administrative rules have reflected the trend toward due process protection.

The following discussion introduces some of these new due process measures as mandated by provincial and local educational agencies. Two caveats must be kept in mind while reading the discussion.

The initial caveat is that unless otherwise indicated, the discussion cannot be generalized to other regions. Second, because a teacher's power over student discipline (*chengjie*) is not directly defined in Chinese law, it is largely unregulated and little due process protection has been required. Therefore, the following discussion is limited to disciplinary sanctions rendered at the school level (*chufen*).

Provisions regarding the rights of students to defend themselves and to hearings are scattered throughout provincial and local rules. Before disciplinary actions can be rendered, the school administrators in the Hunan province must provide students and their parents or guardians opportunities to tell their sides of the stories.[33] The Department of Education of Shandong province requires elementary and secondary schools to have a hearing system in place.[34] A rule issued by the Education Bureau of Qingdao, a city in the Shandong province, specifies how to request hearings, who are allowed to participate, and what rights students have in the process.[35]

Notification of parents is a common requirement in China. Insofar as elementary and secondary school students are largely minors, it is generally required for parents to be notified of their disciplinary sanctions against their children. This notification is mandated by a Ministry of Education regulation[36] as well as many provisional administrative rules.[37] Usually, parents are notified of the sanction after the school authorities reach their decisions. However, in Shanghai, parents are to become involved before officials render their disciplinary decisions. As for the form of notification, the law has not specified whether it must be in writing.

Under state law, students have the right to make external and internal appeals. Even so, this appeal system varies by region. Article 42 of the Education Law (1995) affords students the right to appeal school sanctions via relevant administrative agencies (external appeal).

The Ministry of Education, in 2003, mandated the establishment of a grievance system within the schools (internal appeal).[38] In the Fujian province, junior secondary school students can file external appeals to specified local educational agencies within five days after receiving the sanctions.[39]

In Shanghai, students can choose between an internal grievance system within the school or an external appeal system at the relevant administrative agency.[40] In comparison, senior secondary school students in the Hunan province are advised to first use the internal grievance system. If they still feel aggrieved after the internal review, then students can file external appeals to the education agency in charge of their school.[41]

While the student appeals within these three provinces are discussed as a part of the general student management regulation issued by the provincial department of education, a special regulation on student appeals was passed by the Chongqing municipal government in 2007.[42] This regulation, which defines the external administrative appeal system in Chongqing, is unusual for three reasons.

First, as a regulation enacted by the municipal government directly, it is more powerful than any regulations promulgated by a provincial education agency. Second, as a regulation only dealing with student appeals, it lays out, in great detail, a systematic design for an appeal process. Finally, it covers not only elementary and secondary schools in Chongqing, but also colleges and universities in the region. The creation of this regulation is possibly related to a high-profile legal controversy concerning the expulsion of two college students in the municipality which drew nationwide attention and pushed municipal education officials to seriously consider the necessity of an appeal system.[43]

It is an open question whether judicial remedies are available to students who were subjected to disciplinary actions. According to Article 42 of the Education Law (1995), a student can file a lawsuit if "his or her personal, property, or other legitimate rights or interests have been infringed upon by the school or the teacher."

The wording of the law does not require the exhaustion of grievance or administrative appeals before seeking judicial remedies. In practice, though, Chinese courts sometimes interpret what is at stake in student discipline (even when dealing with expulsions) as the right to education, which is further believed to be distinct from personal or property rights as specified in Article 42. As a result, even though students who suffered personal injuries may sue their schools for tort liability, those who were subjected to school sanctions do not necessarily have a recognized cause of action.

SPECIAL CONSIDERATIONS IN STUDENT DISCIPLINE

Education and Discipline

The wording of the law in China emphasizes the importance and purpose of education in potential situations of student discipline. On the one hand, misbehaving students should be provided help in order to improve their behavior and sanctions must be used sparsely.[44] On the other hand, for those who received sanctions, school authorities should pay special attention to helping and educating children.[45] In other words, education is the goal and a sanction is only a necessary method to achieving that goal ultimately.

Revocation of Sanction

Consistent with the emphasis on their educational purpose, sanctions can be revoked if students have shown significant improvement in their behavior.[46] In China, personal dossiers accompany persons for their entire whole life, from educational institutions to employment. After the revocations, the disciplinary records are removed from the student's personal dossier so that the stigmatizing effect of a disciplinary action can be reduced. This removal provides students who were disciplined with incentives to monitor their behavior.

School, Family, and Community

School authorities should work with families and the community in regard to helping misbehaving students. Parents should provide the "necessary conditions" so that minors can receive their educations[47] and all sectors of society should cultivate good environments for the development of the children and students.[48]

In some areas of China, systematic dropout prevention programs have been put into place. In Xiamen, Fujian province, for instance, if new junior secondary school students do not show up to school within seven days after the registration dates, then the teachers in charge of the students' classes should visit their home three times in the next two weeks.

If students still do not attend class, then it becomes the duty of officials of the township governments or subdistrict offices governing the residence areas of children to ensure their enrollment.[49] In Beijing, school authorities must notify students' parents in truancy situations. If students frequently arrives late or are truant, then educators must discuss this issue with the parents to help the children improve their behavior. If students of compulsory education age are truant for a whole week, then officials must notify the township government or subdistrict office, which will order the parents to send their child to school.[50]

DISCUSSION AND FUTURE DIRECTIONS

This chapter examined practices for student misconduct in China from educational and legal perspectives. Chinese law introduced formal school sanctions as provided for in the regulations and rules of the government as well as the informal disciplinary measures used by teachers.

This chapter sketched the national landscape and, at the same time, highlighted local variations on the rules and regulations. Hopefully, the chapter, through its systematic analysis and special attention to potential Chinese distinctiveness, makes comparison with other countries in this book evident, thus contributing to the search for "best" practices for student misconduct worldwide.

Practices for student misconduct in China are best understood against the backdrop of the country's Confucian heritage culture. The traditional emphasis on appropriate order and discipline may have contributed to the comparatively low prevalence of student misconduct in China.

The notion of helping students improve their behaviors as the primary goal of the discipline and the possibility of removing sanctions records from individuals' personal dossiers may also reflect the Confucian ideas of moral cultivation and education. On the other hand, if the strong disciplining power of schools and teachers in the Confucian tradition go unchecked, the rights of students may be jeopardized.

Max Weber's authority theory[51] is helpful in regard as a means of illustrating the nature of student discipline power. In a traditional society, the power of student discipline was best captured by what Weber called "positional authority" and "charismatic authority." In traditional China, although it cannot be denied that many teachers possessed a good deal of charisma and were, thus, respected by their students, it was their positional power that fundamentally defined the teacher-student relationship.

The relation between teachers and students in China has been compared to the father-son relationship. Given the special position of teachers, students should respect them and follow their commands. In a situation of disobedience, discipline could then be imposed.

When student discipline became regulated by law, in the modern period, "legal-rational" authority entered the picture. Students accepted the discipline against them not simply or not because they thought their teachers had the power to discipline them or they trusted the teachers, but insofar as the discipline was being carried out in accordance with the law.

The reestablishment of the legal system after the Cultural Revolution and the enactment of various educational statutes, regulations, and rules over the past thirty years have helped to define student discipline in legal terms. As China moves toward the "rule of law," the legal-rational authority will become more significant.

As the laws pertaining to student discipline are still developing in China, two aspects of this evolution deserve special attention. First, due process measures have already been mandated in college student discipline throughout China. These measures are also available in elementary and secondary school in the specified regions reviewed in this chapter. To better safeguard students' rights, due process protection should become a general legal requirement in all student discipline. Second, as discussed earlier, the disciplining power of teachers is largely absent in the current legal landscape. Therefore, it is up to the positional authority, possibly coupled with charismatic authority, to supply legitimacy to teachers' actions.

CONCLUSION

Legal regulations do not necessarily lead to good education. Yet, in a modern society, when the disciplinary power of teachers is devoid of legal legitimacy, two risks arise. First, the possibility exists that such unchecked disciplining power can be abused, especially when moral solidarity shatters. Second, when education is increasingly regulated by law, a legal vacuum on this issue may make teachers vulnerable to legal challenges.

Appropriate classroom management actions may be mistaken by students and their parents as a form of corporal punishment (*bianxiang tifa*), for which teachers can be rendered liable. Therefore, future revisions of the educational laws in China need to take the teachers' disciplining power into consideration.

KEY POINTS

1. School authorities are afforded by the Educational Law the power to impose sanctions on misbehaving students. Informal methods of discipline are also used by teachers, which is traditionally and legally considered as part of teachers' rights afforded by the Teacher Law to conduct teaching and educational activities and to guide students' study and development in school.
2. Severe types of discipline which may terminate students' status in schools are excluded from application to children in compulsory education stages.
3. Corporal punishment as discipline is clearly banned by the law, but "convert corporal punishment" does exist in daily education practice and is still beyond definition as a legal term.
4. Subject to local regulations and rules, students in elementary or secondary school may have due process protection in discipline. Adoption of these measures is expected to expand with the development of "rule of law" in China.

NOTES

1. Part of the research for this chapter is supported by the Program for New Century Excellent Talents in University (Project Number: NCET-10-0798).
2. Education Law, art. 14–15 (1995).
3. Art. 46.
4. Compulsory Education Law, art. 2 (2006).
5. Ibid., art. 11.
6. Ibid., art. 2.
7. General Principles of the Civil Law, art. 11–12 (1986).
8. Ibid., art. 16.
9. Tort Liability Law, art. 32 (2009). If the guardians have fulfilled their duties as guardians, their tort liability may be mitigated.
10. Ibid.
11. Richard Jessor et al., "Adolescent Problem Behavior in China and the United States: A Cross-National Study of Psychosocial Protective Factors," *Journal of Research on Adolescence* 13, 329(2003); Ellen Greenberger et al., "The Perceived Social Contexts of Adolescents' Misconduct: A Comparative Study of Youths in Three Cultures," *Journal of Research on Adolescence* 10 (2000). The first study found that U.S. youths engage in more misconduct than Koran youths and Korean youths engage in more misconduct than Chinese youths.
12. Jiliang Shen et al., "Chinese Elementary School Teachers' Perceptions of Students' Classroom Behaviour Problems," *Educational Psychology* 29, 187(2009).
13. Meixia Ding et al., "Chinese Teachers' Perceptions of Students' Classroom Misbehaviour," *Educational Psychology* 28, 305(2008).
14. Shen et al; Ding et al. In contrast, "talking out of turn" is the most prevalent form of behavior problem in Western classrooms.

15. Shen et al; Xianchen Liu and Kurita Hiroshi, "Behavioral and Emotional Problems in Chinese Children: Teacher Reports for Ages 6 to 11," *Journal of Child Psychology and Psychiatry and Allied Disciplines* 41, 253(2000); Jiliang Shen, Zhongguo Zhongxiaoxuesheng Xuexi yu Xinli Fazhan Zhuangkuang Baogao [Report on the Learning and Psychological Development of Elementary and Secondary Students in China] (Beijing: Normal University Press, 2007).

16. Jessor et al; Tao Xin et al., "The Structure of Self-Reported Problem Behaviors in Chinese Children," *Psychology in the Schools* 40, 19(2003); Xianchen Liu et al., "Prevalence and Risk Factors of Behavioral and Emotional Problems Among Chinese Children Aged 6 through 11 Years," *Journal of the American Academy of Child and Adolescent Psychiatry* 38(1999).

17. Shen et al.; Hui Feng et al., "Sociodemographic Correlates of Behavioral Problems among Rural Chinese Schoolchildren," *Public Health Nursing* 28(2011).

18. Qipei Zuo, *Guanyu zhongxiaoxuesheng wenti xingwei de yanjiu* [Behavior Problems of Elementary and Secondary Schoold Students], Xinlixue Tanxin [Outlook in Psychology] 94(1985).

19. Shen et al.

20. Art. 28.

21. Commission of Education, Xiaoxue guanli guicheng [Regulation on Elementary School Management], art. 15 (1996); Ministry of Education, Guanyu gaozhong jianli xuesheng dang'an de zanxing guiding [Temporary Regulation on Establishing Student Dossiers in Senior Secondary Schools] (1984); Commission of Education, Putong zhongdeng zhuanye xuexiao xuesheng xueji guanli guiding [Regulation on Student Record Management in Specialized Secondary Schools], art. 38 (1994); Department of Education of Shandong Province, Shandong sheng zhongxiaoxue xueji guanli guiding [Regulation on Student Record Management in Shandong Province], art. 30 (2007).

22. See, e.g., Department of Education of Human Province, Hunan sheng putong gaozhong xuesheng xueji guanli banfa [Regulation on General Senior Secondary School Student Record Management in Hunan Province], art. 33 (2009).

23. Compulsory Education Law, art. 27, 57 (2006); Minor Protection Law, art. 18 (2006).

24. Commission of Education of Shanghai, Shanghai shi zhongxiaoxue xueji guanli banfa [Regulation on Student Record Management in Elementary and Secondary Schools in Shanghai], art. 47(2006).

25. Dong Zhu, *Qing jiazhang de yishu* [the art of using a teacher-parent conference], Zhongguo jiaoshi bao [China Teacher Newsapaper] December 10, 2003.

26. Art. 29.

27. Art. 21.

28. Art. 37.

29. Teacher Law, art. 37 (1993).

30. Lao Kaisheng and Sun Yunxiao, Xin jiaodian: dangdai zhongguo shaonian ertong renshen shanghai yanjiu baogao [A Research Report on the Personal Injury of Juvenile in Contempoary China] (Beijing: Normal University Press, 2002).

31. Rui Mao et al., *Zhongxiaoxuesheng jilv chufen zhuangkuang yanjiu* [A study on disciplinary action of elementary and secondary school students], Qingnian Yanjiu [Youth Studies] 6(2004).

32. An English translation of this decision is available at *Chinese Education and Society*, vol. 39, no. 3 (2006): 59–69.

33. Department of Education of Human Province, Hunan sheng putong gaozhong xuesheng xueji guanli banfa [Regulation on General Senior Secondary School Student Record Management in Hunan Province], art. 33 (2009).

34. Department of Education of Shandong Province, Shandong sheng putong zhongxiaoxue xueji guanli guiding (shixing) [Regulation on Student Record Management in General Elementary and Secondary Schools in Shandong Province (in trial)], art. 30 (2007).

35. Education Bureau of Qingdao, Zhongxiaoxue chufen zanxing guiding [Provisional Regulation on Student Discipline in Elementary and Secondary Schools], art. 13 (2002). It must be noted that such a hearing in Qingdao is conducted after the decision to take disciplinary action

has been made. So, the hearing is to review, instead of to consider, the disciplinary action. It is different from the pre-decision hearing requirement in the discipline process of college students in Beijing. See Commission of Education of Beijing, Guanyu putong gaodeng xuexiao xuesheng weiji chufen chengxu de ruogan guiding (shixing) [Provisions on the Procedures of Student Discipline in General Higher Education Institutions (in Trial)], art. 17–24 (2005).

36. Commission of Education, Zhongxiaoxue deyu gongzuo guicheng [Regulation on Moral Education in Elementary and Secondary School], art. 27 (1998).

37. See, e.g., Regulation on Student Record Management in Elementary and Secondary Schools in Shanghai, art. 47 (2006); Regulation on Student Record Management in General Elementary and Secondary Schools in Shandong Province (in trial), art. 30 (2007).

38. Ministry of Education, Jiaoyubu guanyu jiaqiang yifazhixiao gongzuo de ruogan yijian [Several Opinions on Strengthening Rule of Law in School] (2003).

39. Department of Education of Fujian Province, Fujiansheng putong chuji zhongxue xueji guanli banfa [Regulation on Student Record Management in Junior Secondary School in Fujian Province], art. 35 (2007).

40. Regulation on Student Record Management in Elementary and Secondary Schools in Shanghai, art. 47 (2006).

41. Regulation on General Senior Secondary School Student Record Management in Hunan Province, art. 35 (2009).

42. Chongqing Municipality, Chongqing shi xuesheng shensu banfa [Regulation on Student Appeal in Chongqing] (2007).

43. Ran Zhang, *Confrontation or Cooperation: Spaces of Action for Student Grievance in Chinese Universities* (2009) (Unpublished PhD dissertation, Indiana University).

44. See, i.e., Regulation on Student Record Management in Elementary and Secondary Schools in Shanghai, art. 47 (2006); Regulation on Student Record Management in Junior Secondary School in Fujian Province, art. 32, 35 (2007); Regulation on General Senior Secondary School Student Record Management in Hunan Province, art. 33 (2009).

45. See, i.e., Regulation on Student Record Management in Elementary and Secondary Schools in Shanghai, art. 48 (2006).

46. Temporary Regulation on Establishing Student Dossiers in Senior Secondary Schools (1984); Regulation on Student Record Management in Specialized Secondary Schools, art. 42 (1994);

47. Education Law, art. 49 (1995).

48. Ibid., art. 45.

49. Bureau of Education of Xiamen City, Xiamenshi putong chuji zhongxue xueji guanli banfa [Regulation on Student Record Management in Junior Secondary School in Xiamen], Art. 5 (2007).

50. Commission of Education of Beijing, Beijing shi zhongxiaoxuexiao xuesheng guanli banfa [Regulation on Student Management in Elementary and Secondary Schools in Beijing], art. 7 (2010).

51. Max Weber, *The Theory of Social and Economic Organization* (New York: Free Press, 1947).

Chapter Three

The Law Regulating Student Discipline in Malaysia

Fatt Hee Tie

In Malaysia, the written Federal Constitution is the primary source of law governing the system of education.[1] The Federal Constitution sets out the legal rights and obligations of all citizens as it represents the supreme law of the country.

Article 4(1) of the Federal Constitution reiterates that even though inconsistency may arise as to which law is more significant, it remains the supreme law of the federation and any law passed after independence which is inconsistent with its provisions shall to the extent of the inconsistency be deemed to be void. Hence, in this respect, the doctrine of constitutional supremacy is clearly laid down in the Federal Constitution.

Historically, the British colonial administration ruled the country for a number of years. The British presence had an impact on the development of the law in what was then known as Malaya. As a consequence, the common law exerts a significant influence on the legal system in Malaysia.

Since Malaysia achieved independence from the British on August 31, 1957, the principles of the common law have been duly recognized and accepted as an integral part of Malaysian law. For the past fifty years, Malaysian judges have exercised wide discretion in importing English common law, equity, and statutes into the legal system when there is a lacuna in Malaysian law. In cases involving litigation in schools, the judiciary has applied English common law in a wide scope.

Among the fundamental liberties guaranteed by the Federal Constitution that are relevant and applicable to school law, in particular, student discipline are equality before the law and equal protection from the law; the right to receive an education; freedom to profess, practice, and propagate religion;

and freedom of speech and expression. Most of the litigation on student discipline has focused on these fundamental liberties.

Besides the Federal Constitution, another source of law regulates the education system as a whole. This particular set of legislation is enacted by Parliament. One significant piece of legislation that has an important impact on the education system is the Education Act of 1996.[2]

The preamble to the Education Act of 1996 expressed the purpose of education as being designed to enable students to have a command of knowledge, skills, and values needed in a competitive and global environment. Further, the act specifies that the education system seeks to develop the full potential of individuals in a holistic and integrated manner from the intellectual, spiritual, emotional, and physical aspects. The act also strives to produce citizens who are responsible, knowledgeable, competent, possess high moral standards, and capable of achieving a high personal well-being.

Under section 19 of the Education Act of 1996, school authorities have the obligation to prepare students for public examinations. Consequently, all students have the right to study in environments that are safe from physical and emotional threats. Students have the right to receive their education and to sit for the public examinations.

Decisions depriving students of this right to pursue their education and prepare for the public examinations through sanctions such as suspensions and expulsions have serious consequences because they can impact their future livelihoods. The long-term effect of these sanctions on students must be considered carefully prior to making a decision.

There is also a third set of legislation known as subsidiary or delegated legislations. These legislations are made by individuals such as the Minister of Education. The powers are conferred on these individuals by an act of Parliament.[3]

In addition, the Ministry of Education (Ministry) issues procedural and administrative guidelines related to school management and governance from time to time. These guidelines, known as professional administrative circulars, are sent to schools occasionally.

The guidelines contain provisions concerning the management of issues related to student management such as corporal punishment, proper school attire, attendance, the ban on hand phones in school, and the correct procedure to be followed when dealing with student discipline. All public schools must abide by the provisions in the professional administrative circulars.

Generally, the Federal Constitution, the educational legislations enacted by Parliament, delegated legislations, and the Ministry's professional administrative guidelines, act to ensure that the system of education operates in a closely regulated as well as bureaucratized environment. The remainder of this chapter reviews the court structure in Malaysia, the state of student misconduct in schools and various topics, and emerging issues. The chapter ends with a brief conclusion.

THE COURT STRUCTURE IN MALAYSIA

The Courts of Judicature Act 1964 sets out the jurisdiction and powers of the Superior Courts under the Malaysian judicial hierarchy.[4] The Superior Courts consists of the Federal Court (the apex court), the Court of Appeal, and the High Court.

Article 121 of the Federal Constitution identifies two High Courts of coordinate jurisdiction and status, the High Court of Malaya and the High Court of Sabah and Sarawak. The Subordinate Courts Act 1948 stipulates the jurisdiction and power of the subordinate courts comprised of the Sessions, Magistrates, and *Penghulu* (head of the village) courts.

In civil cases, parents can appeal to the courts for reinstatement of their children to schools when they disagree with the actions of educational authorities who expel students. Most of the actions taken by parents against educational authorities involved alleged violations of the natural principles of natural justice and challenged as *ultra vires*. Actions can commence at the Sessions Court with appeals to the High Court.

When either parents or school authorities are not satisfied with the orders of the High Court, they can seek review by the Court of Appeal. The subsequent and final appeal is made to the apex court, the Federal Court.

The Federal Court can grant leave in accordance with section 97 of the Courts of Judicature Act 1964: (a) from any judgment or order of the Court of Appeal in respect of any civil cause or matter decided by the High Court in the exercise of its original jurisdiction, and (b) from any decision as to the effect of any provisions of the Constitution including the validity of any written law relating to such provision.

THE STATE OF STUDENT MISCONDUCT IN MALAYSIAN SCHOOLS

As at January 31, 2011, 5.33 million students in Malaysia are enrolled in both primary and secondary schools. The number of teachers in both primary and secondary schools is about 400,000.[5] The teacher-student ratio is large and needs to be improved to ensure more effective learning environments. The low number of teachers also impacts the ability of the school authorities to manage student discipline since more time, energy, and effort is expended to maintain discipline.

Student misconduct continues to be one of the most persistent problems in Malaysian schools. As in many other countries, schools in Malaysia face similar difficulties in coping with the gradual increase in cases involving student misconduct.

Student misconduct is a growing problem in both primary and secondary schools as the number and severity of incidents of misbehavior such as vandalism, theft, gangsterism, and violence committed have increased. Widespread media coverage of student misconduct has further exacerbated the problem. Public awareness of the problem has also risen as a result of wide publicity in the media. An appropriate strategy to address the issue of student misconduct is needed to maintain safe learning environments.

In 1999, in response to public demand for safer schools, the Educational Planning and Policy Research Division of the Ministry conducted a study on gang activities in Malaysian schools. The research report, "A Study on Gangsterism in Daily Secondary Schools"[6] represents a significant step to identify the sources, activities, and membership of student gangs. The study revealed that students' participation in delinquent activities is influenced by three main factors, namely their ethnicity, peer groups, and places of residence.

Students with low parental income who live in densely populated areas, new villages, apartments, or temporary public housing tend to be most at risk. The study showed that at-risk students have a tendency to rebel, break rules and regulations, desire to be the center of attention, have low academic achievement, receive little parental attention, and are susceptible to negative peer influence.

In 2004, the Ministry revealed that there were 249 reports on cases of students' misconduct. The Ministry's statistics reported that there has been a decline in the number of incidences related to bullying and gangsterism in school. Unfortunately, the nature of the misconduct in recent year has changed as it has become more extreme and violent in nature.

The Most Frequent Forms of Student Misconduct

Truancy, bullying, theft, bringing banned items to school such as hand phones, and joining a gang outside school, are the most frequent forms of student misconduct. The other minor offences consist of coming to school late, absence from school due to reasons besides health, not completing assigned homework, willful disobedience to teachers' instruction, and disruptive behavior in class.

The Application of Due Process to Disciplinary Methods

Under the common law doctrine of *in loco parentis*, educational authorities have a legal obligation to ensure that students are safe while in school. Educational authorities are vested with the authority to maintain discipline to protect students from being the victims of misconduct while at the same time ensuring that the teaching learning process continues smoothly.

School officials have the authority to prescribe their own set of rules and regulations to maintain the legitimate interest of all students.[7] The rules and regulations must be fair and reasonable. Disciplinary rules and regulations that violate the fundamental rights set out in the Federal Constitution are *ultra vires*.[8]

Most of parental actions challenging the decisions of school disciplinary authorities focus on the procedures rather than the substance of rules. In addition, the nature of the sanction imposed is seldom challenged.[9] It is mandatory for students (and their parents) to comply with procedures that are more formal when severe penalties are imposed such as expulsions from school. In most instances, a minimal amount of due process is necessary for minor punishments. Nevertheless, all disciplinary actions must comply strictly with the due process procedure to ensure the principle of natural justice is upheld.

Methods of Dealing with Student Discipline

Traditionally, school authorities have adopted a form of preventative strategy to overcome student misconduct. The Ministry disseminates a comprehensive set of school rules and regulations related to student discipline applicable in all schools. These rules and regulations cover school attire, the system of demerit points, the classification of minor and serious offences, and the type of sanctions.

School authorities must provide all students with their own copies of these rules and regulations. Moreover, the rules and regulations are posted in all classrooms, staff room, and on school notice boards. During weekly school assemblies, most officials remind students to abide by the rules and regulations. All teachers are required to understand the various administrative circulars related to school discipline.

School rules are enforced using a system of surveillance, penalties, and punishments ranging from demerit points, corporal punishment, alternative school placement, suspension, and, expulsion. This discussion focuses on three main types of punishments in Malaysian schools: corporal punishment, suspensions, and expulsions.

Enforcement of Corporal Punishment

The Ministry allows corporal punishment or caning to be enforced in schools. Historically, corporal punishment originated during the British colonial administration of the country in the 1950s. It is now an established form of discipline based on the general presumption that to spare the rod would in turn spoil the child. Educational authorities subscribe to the belief that corporal punishment is required to maintain discipline and order in schools. These authorities deem corporal punishment to be effective because it continues to serve important educational interests.

Corporal punishment is administered only when students commit severe acts of misconduct such as taking part in a fist fight or intentionally causing physical damage to school property. Although corporal punishment is permitted, due process is required and officials must take a variety of factors into account before it can be administered.

Among these considerations when thinking about the use of corporal punishment are the type and nature of the misconduct; students' ages and physical sizes; mental capacity of those who misbehave; and the disciplinary history and family background. All principals and teachers must be aware of these factors as applied to corporal punishment along with the policies of their schools and the Ministry.

The Ministry has established a clear set of regulations related to the imposition of corporal punishment. This punishment can be enforced in schools subject to strict and specific conditions. According to Section 5(1) of the Education (School Discipline) Regulations 1959, corporal punishment can only be enforced on boys. It stipulates that:

> For the purposes of maintaining discipline among pupils, the head teacher shall have power to inflict such ordinary school punishments, as may be necessary or expedient.
> Provided that:
> (1) (a) corporal punishment of girl pupils is prohibited, and,
> (b) corporal punishment of boys by a teacher or member of the staff shall be limited to blows with a light cane on the palm of the hand or on the buttocks over the clothes, and shall be inflicted only by the head teacher, or by his express authority given in the specific case.
> (2) A record of all punishments inflicted under paragraph (1) shall be kept confidentially in a form approved by the Registrar.[10]

School principals are the only persons who have the right to cane students. However, principals can delegate the task to teachers who act on their behalf. The teacher representatives are usually the school discipline teachers. Before this can occur, principals must issue official appointment letters authorizing discipline teachers to carry out the punishment.

Official appointment letters are important because they serve vital purposes to prevent allegations of abuse of power by other teachers, particularly when corporal punishment is conducted by those who were not appointed officially by their principals. Letters of authorization issued to teachers to cane students officially show that principals have given consent to official appointees. As such, the letters prevent other teachers from caning students without the express permission of their principals.[11]

Caning is conducted in closed environments rather than at open school assemblies. In fact, caning is usually carried out in principals' offices. Further, caning is restricted to specific body parts, either on the palms of the hands or on students' buttocks. Only reasonable force is allowed. Also, the number of strokes, ranging from one to three, that can be inflicted depends on the severity of the offences.

The Ministry strictly prohibits the use of excessive force as a form of cruel and unusual punishment to protect students from unreasonable and excessive force by school authorities. Teachers who violate the guidelines face disciplinary action from the Ministry's Disciplinary Board. Besides, parents are likely to sue teachers for abuse of power and for the offence of assault under the criminal law.

Under the same regulation, the Ministry requires all principals and teachers to be aware of the purpose of corporal punishment. Public school principals or their appointed representatives are allowed to inflict corporal punishment that is reasonably necessary for the proper education and discipline of students.

The regulation reiterates that the primary purpose of corporal punishment is to educate students and that it is deemed necessary for the training and control of children. Corporal punishment must be performed in a reasonable manner and in good faith that cannot be used to degrade or inflict unduly severe physical abuse on students who misbehave.

The Ministry deals severely with teachers who impose corporal punishment that is cruel and excessive in nature. As noted earlier, these teachers can face both civil and criminal liability because under common law students have the right not to be subjected to excessive corporal punishment in school. If punishment is proved to be excessive, the school authorities may also be liable in damages to students.

Excessive corporal punishment may thus amount to the criminal offence of assault under the Penal Code. At the same time, if there is evidence to show malice, the offender may be subject to other criminal penalties. Hence, the common law acts as an effective restraint to remedy and deter such excesses.

Consequently, the likelihood of civil or criminal proceedings deters unnecessary or excessive corporal punishment because its application must comply with due process of the law. Further, the prior notice and informal hearings requirements associated with corporal punishment are important administrative safeguards necessary to protect against decisions that are *mala fide*.

Procedural Guidelines Concerning Corporal Punishment

Prior to the enforcement of corporal punishment, school principals must comply with the following procedure:

a. inform all teachers and students about the Ministry's policy on corporal punishment;
b. inform all parents about the policy and procedures related to corporal punishment;
c. conduct a hearing and keep a proper record of the proceeding;
d. ensure that the students are informed of the reason why they are to be caned;
e. the punishment must be conducted in a closed environment, specifically in the principal's office;
f. the punishment must be administered by the principal or an appointed representative who is not directly involved in the conflict;
g. another teacher must be present as a witness;
h. the parents receive an official letter from the principal about the punishment;
i. ensure that all the correct procedures are followed;
j. a record of the corporal punishment must be kept and properly documented with the name of the student; nature, time, place and other relevant details of the misconduct; the official complainant; the name of the person who administered the caning and details such as date, place, time; name of witnesses present during the punishment; and, the document is signed.

Suspensions and Expulsions

Suspensions or exclusions of students for short periods of time are often employed to maintain school discipline. Suspensions range from one to three days. However, this punishment has serious repercussions as they are deprived of the fundamental right to receive an education even though it is temporary in nature.

School principals must consider three important issues before they suspend or expel students: the pedagogical effect on students who may face difficulties keeping up with what has been taught during the periods of their absences from school; decisions to suspend or expel may have elements of bias and discrimination; and, whether the rules of natural justice have been complied with when actions are taken.

The due process clause of the Federal Constitution of Malaysia in Article 5(1) reads: "no person shall be deprived of his life or personal liberty save in accordance with law." As in other jurisdictions such as the United States and

England, these due process rights initially applied only to individuals charged with criminal offences.

Yet, the two cases of *Mahadevan*[12] and *Meor Atiqulrahman*[13] changed this traditional approach in Malaysia. Malaysian courts in both cases ruled that insofar as students possessed liberty and property interests in attending school, they had to receive some due process protections before the right was taken away. Put another way, the courts agreed that it is unconstitutional to allow school administrators to deprive students of their rights to an education without hearings of any kind because doing so violates the procedural due process provision of the Federal Constitution.

Decisions to temporarily suspend or exclude permanently from school must be made only after a proper and fair hearing in light of Malaysian law providing a free, compulsory education for all students between the ages of six and twelve. In this regard, Regulation 4 of the Education (School Discipline) Regulations 1959 expressed clearly that the head of a school is the person who is fully responsible for the overall discipline of a school.

In the Malaysian context, the head at a primary school is known as the headmaster or headmistress. At the secondary school level, this person is known as the principal. Whether headmaster or headmistress or principal, these educators are fully responsible for student discipline.

Under Regulation 8, a head teacher can exercise any of the two options: suspend or expel students. Either way, it is mandatory for educators to follow the relevant regulations before acting to suspend or expel students.

Before issuing orders to suspend or expel students, head teachers must be satisfied that their actions are going to be effective and desirable to maintain school discipline. In most cases, the term "desirable" tends to be interpreted in an objective manner. It may be tantamount to reasonableness. As set out in the regulations, only the head teacher has the authority to suspend or expel a student.

Returning to the litigation, in *Mahadevan*'s[14] case, the trial commenced at the High Court in Seremban, proceeded to the Federal Court in Kuala Lumpur,[15] and was finally resolved by the then highest court of appeal at that time, the Privy Council in the United Kingdom.[16]

The case arose when the headmaster expelled a student due to repeated acts of misconduct. During this time the headmaster called the student to his office to investigate the allegations he faced and warned him about the probability of expulsion. The student applied for two declarations. First, the student sought a declaration that the order of expulsion made by the headmaster and subsequently confirmed by the school's Board of Governors, was null, void, and of no effect. Second, the plaintiff applied for an order seeking reinstatement as a pupil of the school.

The High Court in Seremban allowed both applications, finding that a mere warning by the headmaster that the student might have been expelled did not comply with the principles of natural justice. Under the circumstances, the court was of the opinion that the headmaster failed to provide adequate notice to allow the plaintiff to appreciate the exact nature and purpose of the interview at his office.

At the same time, the court noted that the headmaster had sufficient evidence related to the plaintiff's misconduct to justify the expulsion and exercised the power to expel honestly and in good faith. Still, the court was convinced that the headmaster's failure to provide adequate notice to the student deprived him of a fair opportunity of being heard.

On further review, the headmaster successfully appealed to the Federal Court in Kuala Lumpur. The court focused on whether the correct procedure was followed. The court duly recognized that Regulation 8 of the Education (School Discipline) Regulations 1959 vested the headmaster with a quasi-judicial function but it did not expressly prescribe a special form of procedure.

Under these circumstances, the court explained that the headmaster was free to determine the type of procedure subject to the condition that some form of inquiry occurred consistent with the rules of natural justice. Of far more significance is that the Federal Court reiterated that a headmaster cannot be expected to conduct elaborate inquiries before rendering orders to expel pupils. In explicating the need for inquiries, the court pointed out that schools come under the category of that vast area where the principle of *audi alteram partem* (literally, "hear the other party too") can only be applied under the most general considerations.

The pupil then appealed to the Privy Council which held that the rules of natural justice require headmasters to act fairly by allowing students to know the complaint about their alleged misconduct and be given opportunities to be heard. Their Lordships emphasized that there is no substance in the contention that the rules of natural justice required the headmaster to tell the student specifically that he intended to expel him unless he had provided a satisfactory explanation of the misconduct which was the subject of the interview.

In the judgment, Lord Diplock expressed that in relation to such administrative matters as the expulsion of a pupil from a school it would be inappropriate to model the procedure on that of a criminal trial.[17] The Privy Council thus upheld the student's expulsion.

Procedural Requirements Concerning Suspensions and Expulsions

Suspensions are used to punish students for infractions including truancy or absences from school without medical letters, bullying, and repeated misconduct such as smoking in schools. Prior to suspension, schools authorities must provide a minimum due process.

The procedural due process for student suspension includes:

a. provide students with written notice of the misconduct and the intended punishment(s);
b. allow students opportunities to refute the charges;
c. provide evidence to show the misconduct;
d. conduct hearings before impartial disciplinary committees;
e. inform parents via a written notice of the decision to suspend and the duration of the suspension; and
f. must ensure that parents respond in writing that they are aware of the duration of the suspensions of their children.

Given the severity of the punishment, school authorities must provide students facing expulsions more elaborate procedural safeguards when compared with those who are facing suspensions. *Mahadevan*'s[18] case acts as an important reference when decisions are made to suspend or expel students from school, highlighting the fact that principals must comply with procedural due process.

Expulsions are imposed for major infractions including violence against peers or other school personnel, theft, assault, possession of a weapon, drug abuse, and participation in criminal activity. Insofar as expulsion is permanent in nature, students must receive procedural protection before they can be excluded from school.

The steps for procedural due process for student expulsions are as follows:

a. ensure that principals (or headmasters) provide written clear notice of the allegations of misconduct to students and their parents;
b. the notice to suspend or expel must be clear and specific;
c. the allegations must specify the types of misconduct, times and places where they were supposedly committed, and the names and signatures of the witnesses who were present;
d. provide an opportunity for students to present evidence and witnesses to rebut the allegations;
e. create independent impartial disciplinary committees for the hearing;
f. inform the students and their parents in writing about the place, time, and circumstances of the hearings;
g. ensure that there is sufficient time for students to prepare their defenses;
h. inform students that they are entitled to their right to representation;
i. ensure that the hearings are fair;
j. principals/headmasters must prepare written record of their decisions; and

k. copies of the decisions must be given to the students, their parents, and all relevant parties.

Student Dress Codes

Malaysian public school students have a common dress code because educational authorities have the legal ability to place restrictions on their dress or attire. The authority granted by the Ministry is based on legitimate educational and safety considerations. Still, the right to restrict students' dress and appearance has seldom been a litigated issue in Malaysia. Neither has it been a major issue for debate.

The Ministry of Education in Malaysia has prescribed a fixed set of school attire for all primary and secondary school students in public school. The dress code is clear, specific, and reasonable. It is mandatory for all students to abide with the strict dress code. To a large extent, the dress code has been effective in reducing the incidences of violence and the presence of gangs in school. At the same time, the dress code has served the legitimate educational purposes of improving safety and decreasing socioeconomic differences among students from various ethnic groups.

As noted, cases related to the dress code brought by parents against the school are rare. The courts are reluctant to interfere with policies and school regulations related to dress code because they deemed that school authorities have the experience and knowledge to deal with such matters.

In other words, the courts recognize that school officials have the right to implement dress code and grooming policies to maintain discipline, prevent disruption to the teaching-learning process, and to ensure that students are safe and free from any forms of disturbances. Consequently, the courts would allow school authorities to establish their own sets of regulations with regard to dress code as long as they are based on legitimate educational objectives.

Nevertheless, the case of *Meor*[19] has been one of the rare disputes that led to litigation. The dispute focuses on the right of students to wear a religious head gear called the "serban" or turban to school. The students claimed that the Federal Constitution guarantees freedom of religion and expression as they sought to assert their rights through their religious attire at school.

The plaintiffs were students at a government primary school where the headmistress established a set of regulations prohibiting pupils from wearing turbans to school. It is important to note that the Ministry's own set of regulations on dress codes did not mention banning turbans from schools. The headmistress expelled the plaintiffs when they refused to follow the regulations despite having provided them with a number of warnings and offering them the advice to comply with the rule.

The plaintiffs raised two issues. First, the students alleged that the headmistress, by establishing her own dress code regulations banning the turban, violated the Ministry's regulations. Second, the plaintiffs claimed that it was their religious right to wear turbans to school; in this regard, the students charged that the headmistress infringed their fundamental right of freedom of religion guaranteed under Article 11(1) of the Federal Constitution, pursuant to which "every person has the right to profess and practice his religion and, subject to clause (4), to propagate it." The students further alleged that wearing a turban is a symbol of practicing one's religion.

After the High Court entered a judgment in favor of the students, the headmistress sought further review from the Court of Appeal in Putrajaya.[20] The main issue on appeal was whether the headmistress, by refusing to permit the students to attend school wearing turbans, violated their "right to profess and practice" their religion under Article 11(1) of the Federal Constitution.

The court applied the test of "integrality" in observing that that the answer lies in whether the right to wear a turban represents an integral part of the religion of Islam. The jurists deemed this a question of fact to be determined by the plaintiffs based on relevant and admissible evidence placed before the court.

Nevertheless, the court found that there was not a shred of evidence to confirm that wearing the turban is mandatory and an integral part of Islam. In addition, the court reasoned that educational institutions are, at common law, entitled to prescribe the appropriate uniforms to be worn by their pupils.

The court further reiterated that the Ministry and individual school headmistresses or principals are vested with the authority to maintain discipline and establish regulations related to the uniforms of schoolchildren. As part of its analysis, the court acknowledged that the judiciary does not interfere in these issues unless there is a breach of the duty to act fairly. Subsequently, the plaintiff pupils appealed to the Federal Court in Putrajaya.

The Federal Court dismissed the appeal on the ground that the School Regulations of 1997 that prohibits students from wearing turbans as part of their uniforms during school hours does not contravene the provisions of Article 11(1) of the Federal Constitution.[21] The court ruled that the restrictive dress code set up by the headmistress was simply not an unconstitutional abridgment of the right to freedom of religion. The court concluded that there was a clear justification for the curtailment of the constitutional right provided under Article 11(1) of the Federal Constitution in enforcing the dress code.

Procedural Requirements Concerning Student Dress Codes

Meor[22] provides significant implications to principals and teachers with respect to rules and regulations related to students' dress code. The procedural requirement that can be drawn from the case include

a. school authorities have the right to establish their own clear set rules and regulations;
b. the rules and regulations set up by educational officials must not contradict with those established by the Federal Constitution, Ministry, and other relevant authorities;
c. educators must ensure that their rules and regulations are clear and specific;
d. school rules should provide for due process before penalties can be imposed;
e. the penalties for offences must be clear and easy to understand; and
f. authorities should provide copies of Ministry's rules and regulations on dress codes to all teachers and students.

EMERGING ISSUES

Two major issues are emerging in Malaysia with regard to student misconduct. The first issue involves the nature of the misconduct as student acts of misbehavior have become increasingly violent in nature. Incidences of fighting that resulted in death in residential schools and fighting have been recorded and placed on the internet by students and others. The Ministry has already implemented some measures to resolve the issue but must do more.

A second emerging issue is cyber-bullying and sex-texting that have emerged as major sources of concern among educators and parents. It is envisaged that such incidences are likely to continue to increase in the near future if appropriate strategies are not implemented to raise awareness among students of the dangerous consequences of their involvement in such activities.

To address both of these issues, Malaysian educational policymakers and lawmakers need to examine the best practices available from other countries. Then, they need to implement policies and procedures designed to protect students from the risks.

CONCLUSION

School discipline is an integral part of training and preparing students to be future law abiding citizens whether in Malaysia or other parts of the world. School principals, headmasters, headmistresses, and teachers are empowered with the authority and duty by the Ministry of Education to regulate student behavior to protect legitimate educational interests. Corporal punishment, suspensions, and expulsions can thus be imposed to achieve this purpose.

In most circumstances, the courts are reluctant to interfere with sanctions that have been reasonably imposed by school officials. Nevertheless, Malaysian courts have demonstrated their willingness to intervene if the decisions of educators are *mala fide*, *ultra vires*, or violate students' constitutionally protected rights.

Simply put, students must be afforded procedural due process prior to being subject to the decisions made by disciplinary committees. Further, students are entitled to more formal procedures if they face serious punishments. As the decisions in both *Mahadevan*[23] and *Meor*[24] demonstrated, principals can be liable for unlawful punishment of students when their actions are deemed *ultra vires*. However, school authorities have considerable latitude in controlling student behavior to safeguard the teaching learning process insofar as reasonable sanctions are necessary to protect the interests of all individuals in schools.

KEY POINTS

1. It is mandatory to comply with the due process and the rules of natural justice in all decisions related to disciplinary actions.
2. Corporal punishment is allowed in schools subject to strict compliance with specific procedures.
3. School authorities must ensure that school rules and regulations are fair, transparent, and stated in a clear manner.
4. Schools are required to adopt a preventative strategy to minimize student misconduct.

NOTES

1. Malaysia, *Federal Constitution*. (2010). Kuala Lumpur: International Law Book Services. The Federal Constitution is a written constitution modeled along the Indian Constitution, which in turn, is based on basic principles of the British government and constitutional conventions. It has been described as based on the "Westminster" model.

2. Malaysia, Education Act 1996 (Act 550). Kuala Lumpur: International Law Book Services.

3. Section 3 of the Interpretation Acts defines subsidiary legislation as "any proclamation, rule, regulation, order, notification, bye-law, or other instrument made under any Act, Enactment, Ordinance, or other lawful authority and having legislative effect." Examples include: Educational Regulations (Special Education), 1997; Educational Regulations (National Curriculum), 1997; and, Educational Regulations (Parent-Teacher Association), 1998.

4. Court of Judicature Act 1964, Kuala Lumpur: International Law Book Services.

5. Malaysia, Ministry of Education, Retrieved May 27, 2011. Available at http://www.moe.gov.my.

6. Malaysia. Ministry of Education, Educational Planning and Policy Research Division. (1999). *Study of Gangsterism in Daily Secondary Schools*, Kuala Lumpur: Ministry of Education.

7. Fatt Hee Tie. (2007). "The Educational Rights of Students in Malaysia." In C. J. Russo, D. J. Stewart, and J. De Groof (eds.). *The Educational Rights of Students: International Perspectives on Demystifying the Legal Issues*. Lanham, MD: Rowman and Littlefield Education.

8. Fatt Hee Tie. (2011). *Education Law in Malaysia: Principles and Practice*. Selangor: Sweet and Maxwell Asia.

9. M. M. McCarthy, N. H. Cambron-McCabe, and S. Thomas, S. (2004). *Legal Rights of Teachers and Students*. Boston: Pearson Education.

10. Malaysia. Ministry of Education. Professional Circular No. 1/1972. Education (School Discipline) Regulations 1959.

11. Malaysia. Ministry of Education. Professional Circular No. KP 0504/11 (144), February 4, 1972.

12. *Mahadevan v. Anandarajan and Ors*. [1970] 1 MLJ 50.

13. *Meor Atiqulrahman bin Ishak dan lain-lain lwn Fatimah bte Sihi dan lain-lain.* [2000] 5 MLJ 375.

14. Supra x.

15. *Anandarajan and Ors. v. Mahadevan.* [1971] 2 MLJ 8.

16. *Mahadevan v. Anandarajan and Ors*. [1974] 1 MLJ 1.

17. Ibid.

18. Supra 10.

19. Supra 11.

20. *Fatimah bte Sihi and Ors. v. Meor Atiqulrahman bin Ishak and Ors*. [2005] 2 MLJ 25.

21. *Meor Atiqulrahman Ishak and Ors. v. Fatimah Sihi and Ors.* [2006] 4 CLJ 1.

22. Ibid.

23. Supra 15.

24. Supra 20.

Chapter Four

Legal Aspects and Practical Application of Disciplinary Actions in the Turkish Public Educational System

Ricardo Lozano and Irem Kızılaslan

Between 2010 and 2011, Turkey experienced an increased level of involvement in and attention from the international community. During this time, Turkey's leaders positioned the nation as a key player and a model to be replicated by the crumbling dictatorships formerly controlling a significant part of the Middle East and Northern Africa. Turkey's strategic location and steady economic growth in the midst of the current worldwide financial crisis have also contributed to its position as an important trade partner between East and West.

Alongside Turkey's rapid economic growth and modernization, in recent years, academic achievement in the country has also undergone significant progress with no apparent major problems to be tackled in the near future. OECD's Program for International Student Assessment's (PISA) 2009 results highlight the fact that students in Turkey made noteworthy progress in reading, science, and mathematics scores in relation to the same scores in 2003.

Turkey's mean score in mathematics rose from 423 in 2003 to 445 in 2009. Likewise, the science mean score increased from 434 to 454 and the reading mean score from 441 to 464 between 2003 and 2009. Among the sixty-five countries assessed in 2009, Turkey ranks forty-third in science and mathematics and forty-first in reading proficiency (PISA, 2009, pp. 41, 44, and 152).

With regard to issues of misbehavior in schools, Turkey does not seem to have a significant problem to be dealt with either. PISA's 2009 results indicate that 74 percent of fifteen-year-old students reported calm classrooms where teachers "never or hardly ever" or "in some lessons" have to wait a long time for students to quiet down (OECD, 2011, p. 2).

Notwithstanding the positive scores pertaining to academics and discipline, in Turkey, approximately 50 percent of children are reported to be subjected to different forms of physical punishment in school. Moreover, the vast majority of teachers in Turkey believe in the need for corporal punishment as an integral part in the development of the child (Gozutok, Er, and Karacaoglu, 2006, p. 232). And despite the fact that corporal punishment is unlawful in Turkey, it is regularly carried out in every grade level in virtually all regions of the country.

Teacher education related to legal foundations of education, classroom management, and modern approaches to discipline is virtually nonexistent in Turkey. Consequently, the country would greatly profit from the integration of educational best practices with regard to the legal aspects of school discipline and classroom management to preservice and inservice teacher education programs. The remainder of this chapter consists of examinations of Turkey's background information; its legal system; summaries of regulations regarding education and discipline; emerging issues; and a conclusion.

NATIONAL BACKGROUND INFORMATION

Location

Turkey is located in both southeastern Europe and southwestern Asia, bordering the Black Sea, between Bulgaria and Georgia, and bordering the Aegean Sea and the Mediterranean Sea, between Greece and Syria. The country is strategically located, with 97 percent of its total land area of 814.578 km^2 in Asia and 3 percent in Europe. Additionally, Turkey controls the Bosporus, Sea of Marmara, and Dardanelles straits that link the Black and Aegean Seas (Yenen, 2011).

Brief History of Major Events

Modern Turkey was founded in 1923 from the Anatolian remnants of the defeated Ottoman Empire by Mustafa Kemal (1881–1938), later honored with the title Atatürk or "Father of the Turks." With the foundation of the Republic in 1923, a considerable reform movement started in many fields, including education, which began to Westernize many of the nation's practices. Under Atatürk's leadership, the country adopted wide-ranging social, legal, and political reforms to achieve social change and modernization, moving from an Islamic entity to a modern secular state.

The transition to the multiparty system in 1950 and military coups in 1960 and 1980 denoted important turning points in the country's history.

Turkey joined the United Nations in 1945 and in 1952 it became a member of NATO. In 1964, Turkey became an associate member of the European Community. Over the past decade, the country has undertaken numerous reforms to strengthen its democracy and economy; Turkey began accession membership talks with the European Union in 2005 (CIA, 2014).

Population

Turkey has a total population of 81,619,322 (2014 estimates), with a median age of 28.5. The country's age structure is as follows: 0–14 years: 25.5 percent; 15–24 years: 16.8 percent; 25–54 years: 42.9 percent; 55–64 years: 6.7 percent; 65 years and over: 8.1 percent (CIA, 2014). Life expectancy at birth in Turkey is 73.29 years, and the total fertility rate is 2.08 children born per woman. The most highly represented ethnic groups in the country are Turkish, 70 percent; Kurdish, 18 percent; and other minorities, 12 percent (2008 estimates; CIA 2014). Turkey is 99.8 percent Muslim, with the remaining 0.2 percent mostly Christian and Jewish. Turkish is the official language, with other minority languages spoken, particularly in the East (CIA, 2014).

AN OVERVIEW OF TURKEY'S LEGAL SYSTEM

Turkey is a republic founded on the principle of the division of powers into legislative, executive and judiciary branches. The primary sources of Turkish law are the constitution, laws, law-amending ordinances, international treaties, regulations, and bylaws (Yazici, 2011); nonetheless, the constitution is the highest body in the Turkish legal system. According to Article 11 of the constitution:

> The provisions of the Constitution are fundamental legal rules binding upon legislative, executive and judicial organs, and administrative authorities and other institutions and individuals. Laws shall not be in conflict with the Constitution.

Article 2 of the constitution enumerates the democratic and secular features of the Republic.

> The Republic of Turkey is a democratic, secular and social state governed by the rule of law, bearing in mind the concepts of public peace, national solidarity and justice respecting human rights, loyal to the Atatürk nationalism and based on the fundamental tenets set forth in the Preamble.

The president is the head of state and is elected by at least two-thirds majority of the Turkish Grand National Assembly (the Meclis), for a one-time, 7 year term. The president heads the National Security Council and represents the office of the Commander in Chief. The executive power is in the hands of the president and the Council of Ministers, which is headed by the prime minister. The prime minister is appointed by the president from among the members of the Turkish Grand National Assembly.

The prime minister nominates ministers whose appointments are subject to the approval of the Turkish Grand National Assembly. The Council of Ministers issues regulations on the application of laws and other matters, provided that they do not conflict with existing laws, and are examined by the Council of State.

The legislative power rests on the Turkish Grand National Assembly (the Meclis), which consists of a 550-seat, unicameral body elected under a system of proportional representation by universal adult suffrage for a five-year term. Only parties which have gathered more than 10 percent of the national vote are represented in the assembly. The Turkish Grand National Assembly enacts, amends, and revokes laws; supervises the work of the Council of Ministers; and authorizes the Council of Ministers to issue decrees on specific matters regarding the rule of law.

The judiciary reviews the constitutionality of laws, decrees, and the rules of procedure of the Turkish Grand National Assembly. Its decisions are published immediately in the official gazette and are binding for all, including the Legislative and Executive powers. Turkey has a unified legal system of civil and military courts, each with a Court of Appeals in Ankara (SE-Times, 2011).

AN OVERVIEW OF REGULATIONS REGARDING EDUCATION

The right to education in Turkey has been secured for all by Article 42 of the constitution, establishing that "no one shall be deprived of the right of learning and education." Turkish education is organized on the basis of the Law of the Organization and Duties of the Ministry of National Education, the Basic Law of National Education, and the laws regulating the education system, as well as development plans, government programs, decision of national education councils, and regulations regarding the principles related to the types, levels, and functions of education (OECD, 2005).

The Basic Law of National Education No. 1739 establishes the aims of the Turkish National Education System:

> To raise all individuals as citizens who are committed to the principles and reforms of Atatürk and to the nationalism of Atatürk as expressed in the Constitution, who adopt, protect and promote the national, moral, human, spiritual and cultural values of the Turkish Nation, who love and always seek to exalt their family, country and nation, who know their duties and respon-

sibilities towards the Republic of Turkey which is a democratic, secular and social state governed by the rule of law, founded on human rights and on the tenets laid down in the preamble to the Constitution, and who have internalized these in their behavior;
To raise them as constructive, creative and productive persons who are physically, mentally, morally, spiritually and emotionally balanced, have a sound personality and character, with the ability to think freely and scientifically and have a broad worldview, that are respectful for human rights, value personality and enterprise, and feel responsibility towards society;
To prepare them for life by developing their interests, talents and capabilities and providing them with the necessary knowledge, skills and attitudes and the habit of working with others and to ensure that they acquire a profession which shall make them happy and contribute to the happiness of society.

REGULATIONS REGARDING DISCIPLINE IN EDUCATION

Laws on promotion, appreciation, and punishment of primary (No. 4357) and secondary (No. 26408) teachers have been decreed in Turkey with the purpose of protecting students against physical and emotional abuse in schools. Corporal punishment has been legally banned from Turkish schools since 1923 (law 1702 and state personnel law 657). Correction guidelines to be exercised in the case of student misbehavior in Turkish schools are also in existence; grades one through five lack legal guidelines, mandates, or laws concerning student discipline.

The disciplinary actions to be taken toward sixth, seventh, and eighth grade students as the result of their involvement in specific reprehensible actions are stated in Regulation 27090 for Primary Education Institutions published in the Official Gazette on December 24, 2008:

> *Verbal Warning*: Late coming, continual absenteeism without an excuse, extending period of permission given by school without an excuse, displaying bad manners.
> *Written Censure*: Arrogant or disrespectful behavior directed toward administrators, teachers, other school staff or students; ignoring school rules and disrupting the learning environment; interrupting school sponsored activities; continual lying, cheating; falsifying official records; disobeying the dress code; smoking; fighting.
> *Expulsion*: Actions against the fundamental principles of the Constitution, sexual assault, insulting, slandering, threatening, carrying weapons within the school premises, misusing school materials, acts of discrimination, damaging the belongings of others, attacking administrators or teachers, promoting the use of alcohol or other habit-forming substances.

The Award and Discipline Regulation for Secondary Education Institutions (No. 26408), published on January 19, 2007, in the *Official Gazette*, establishes the following disciplinary actions to be taken toward secondary school students engaging in the following corresponding reprehensible actions:

> *Written Censure*: Not keeping the school and school materials clean and tidy; failing to fulfill duties required by teachers or administrators; violating the established dress code; smoking; handling the belongings of others without their consent; failing to attend school with all the required supplies; arrogant or disrespectful behavior towards administrators, teachers, or other school staff; disrupting class; cheating.
> *Short-Term Suspension*: Sexual and verbal harassment, insulting, slandering; discriminating against others; insulting teachers, administrators or other staff; fighting; bullying.
> *Expulsion*: Disrespect toward the Turkish flag or any other national or state symbols; denigrating national and spiritual values; insulting these values; theft; damaging of school property; disrupting classes, exams or other activities; use or possession of habit-forming substances; coercing others to engage in illicit activities.
> *Expulsion from Formal Education*: Insulting the Turkish flag or any other national or state symbols; taking individual or collective action against the fundamental principles of the Constitution; organization or involvement in divisive actions with the purpose of discriminating against individuals on the basis of language, ethnicity, sex or political, philosophical and religious beliefs; disrupting the actions of school committees; trading of habit-forming substances; disrupting the learning environment; forming gangs; kidnapping; theft for ransom.

THE STATE OF STUDENT MISCONDUCT IN TURKISH SCHOOLS

The Most Frequent Forms of Student Misconduct

Student misconduct in Turkey may be classified in five categories: misconduct with regards to academic tasks; inappropriate behaviors and attitudes toward teachers; inappropriate behaviors and attitudes toward peers; disregarding school policies' and improper personal behaviors (Siyez, 2009).

The most frequently reported misconduct with regard to academic tasks in Turkish classrooms is speaking out of turn. Additionally, interrupting other students, moving in classrooms, and avoiding responsibilities ("not doing homework" and "not bringing supplies to class") are commonly observed disciplinary problems related to academic tasks in Turkey. Defiance, rudeness, and shouting are inappropriate behaviors and attitudes toward teachers reported in Turkey. However, these behaviors and attitudes are infrequent in Turkish schools. In relation to misbehavior toward other students, the most recurrently reported actions are verbal aggression, physical aggression, swearing, and fighting.

Disregarding school policy has not been observed to be a major issue concerning students in Turkey. Nevertheless, issues of misbehavior regarding this matter are: Arriving late to class, dress code violations, and cheating. Finally, other improper personal behaviors reported by teachers in Turkey include laughing, arriving late to class, not being able to answer teacher's questions, chewing gum, and, most recently, using electronic devices during the time of instruction (Atıcı and Merry, 2001; Aydın, 2010; Boyacı, 2009; Boyraz, 2007; Danaoğlu, 2009; Erol, Ozaydın, and Koç, 2010; Ozben, 2010; Ozkılınc-Nezıhoğlu and Sabancı, 2010; Siyez, 2009; Turnuklu and Galton, 2001).

Issues of misbehavior in Turkish classrooms vary according to the age and socioeconomic status of students. Behaviors such as defiance, rudeness, swearing, and fighting are mostly attributed to older students in grades 8–12 while talking and interrupting teachers and students are behaviors typically associated with younger (primary) students. Moreover, student misbehavior is more frequently observed in public (as opposed to more affluent, private) schools located in regions of the country reported to be of lower socioeconomic status (Akkok, Askar, and Sucuoglu, 1995; Kilimci 2009; Sirkeci, 2010).

Dealing with Misconduct in Schools

The most commonly identified approaches to misconduct issues in Turkey can be classified in three categories: physical; verbal; and time away from instruction. With regard to physical approaches to discipline issues, Turkish culture favors the notion that adults possess the right to punish a misbehaving child and that teachers hold the right to beat the child if he "deserves" it (Turkum, 2010). Thus, corporal punishment is prevalent within both family and school ambits. In Turkey, close to 50 percent of children are subjected to different forms and degrees of corporal punishment in schools. Additionally, most teachers believe in the necessity of physical punishment for the development of the child (Gozutok, Er, and Karacaoglu, 2006, p. 232).

Pupils who are subjected to physical punishment in schools, especially in impoverished areas of the country, consider it "natural" to be subjected to this treatment (Gomleksiz et al., 2008; Kilimci, 2009). The most frequently observed disciplinary methods involving corporal punishment in classrooms in Turkey are slapping, ear pinching, hair pulling, hitting with a ruler, have students stand in one foot for long periods of time, kicking, and punching in the head (Aydın, 2010; Boyacı, 2009; Gomleksiz et al., 2008).

Verbal approaches of discipline are also prevalent in Turkish classrooms. Among the most common forms of this approach to discipline are scolding harshly and referring to students as "retarded," "dog," "stupid," and "imbecile." Also reported, though less frequently as verbal approaches to discipline, are talking to the student, verbal warning, and offering advice regarding ways to overcome the particular misbehavior (Aydın, 2010; Boyacı, 2009; Calışkan Maya, 2004; Erol, Ozaydın, and Koç, 2010; Gomleksiz et al., 2008; Siyez, 2009).

Time away from instruction is another common approach to discipline in Turkish schools. The most regularly observed forms of this discipline approach are: Sending students away from the classroom, referring students to the school administration, and restricting students to looking at waste paper bins and blackboards during the time of instruction (Boyacı, 2009; Calışkan Maya, 2004).

Due Process and Discipline

The Ministry of National Education issued circulars in 1995, 2003, 2005, and 2006 designed to help prevent violence in schools. In accordance with the 2006 circular, a commission should be established in every school with the purpose of developing action plans for the prevention of violence (Turkum, 2010). However, in reality, physical and verbal abuses are prevalent in Turkish schools. In practice, corporal punishment is tolerated, unpunished, and mostly overlooked not only by school teachers and administrators, but also by society as a whole.

The roots of the corporal punishment pervasive in modern Turkish schools can be traced back to the Ottoman period when *falaka* (foot whipping) was a customary practice in the formal education system (Hatipoglu Sumer and Aydın, 1999). Further, Turkish proverbs such as "beating is from heaven," "roses grow wherever a teacher hits," or "one who does not slap his daughter will slap his knees" indicate that corporal punishment is a fundamental component of the authoritarian, long-established culture reflected in today's educational system.

Traditionally, when children are taken to school for the first time, parents say to their teachers: "The flesh belongs to you, the bones to me," thus giving teachers absolute authority over the physical integrity of their children. Due process, understood as the legal requirement that the state must respect all of the legal rights that are owed to a person, then, is virtually nonexistent in Turkish schools.

EMERGING ISSUES

Most issues of misbehavior in Turkish classrooms are mild in nature. Insulting, defiance, and disrespect are infrequently present in Turkish schools. The strong approach that teachers take to discipline in Turkish classrooms coupled with the fact that students are expected to exert absolute obedience to their teachers (Turkum, 2010) are possible contributors to the prevention of major disciplinary problems in the country.

Talking is among the most frequently encountered misbehavior problems in Turkish classrooms. Still, it is important to point out the fact that Turkish teachers are predisposed to be extremely sensitive to talking and even whispering among students. Teacher-centered instruction is the prevailing approach to education in Turkey, where the role of teacher is to dispense facts and the role of the student is to listen and memorize the information. Classroom noises, even when resulting from work or study, is, generally speaking, not tolerated in Turkish schools (Akkok, Askar, and Sucuoglu, 1995; Atıcı and Merry, 2001).

Based on the previously cited research, and our combined years of experience as educators in the country, it is possible to suggest that the particularly minor misbehavior problems common in Turkey are the reflection of a lack of stimulating, thought-provoking, learning environments in schools. Consequently, these problems could possibly be minimized through the introduction of practical, legally sound, approaches to teaching and discipline.

Modern approaches to education address issues of diversity in ways recognizing every individual's right to be educated, despite their particular learning style. Yet, most teaching education programs in Turkey address neither practical concerns related to individual learning styles and classroom management nor practical approaches to issues of misbehavior. It is thus imperative for educational institutions at all levels to address this matter by providing preservice and in-service teacher education programs addressing best practices with regards to discipline and instruction. Also, clear, practical instruction related to the legal foundations of Turkish education is an essential subject to be addressed in teacher education programs in the country.

Generations of educators in Turkey have approached discipline in abusive and violent manners. Most of these educators are unaware of the potential negative legal implications emerging from inappropriate discipline management in schools. The current economic growth and modernization experienced by Turkey must be complemented by the modernization of its educational system and institutions, particularly with regard to reasonable, legal, approaches to discipline in schools.

CONCLUSION

The economic growth and development experienced by Turkey in recent years has contributed to the strengthening of its economy. This progress has also contributed to the development of a more educated society. The fact is clearly seen through the recently increased academic achievement of Turkish students.

Despite the significant progress made by the Turkish economy and society in recent years, remains of the traditional, authoritarian culture prevalent in the Ottoman period are visible in today's education system. An example of the existence of these remains is that, currently, about 50 percent of school age children in Turkey experience corporal punishment as a regular measure of discipline. And while laws and regulations providing for the protection of the emotional and physical integrity of students in schools are in existence in Turkey, the application of corporal punishment in schools is prevalent, thus exposing the fact that these laws and mandates are, essentially, unheeded.

Teacher training programs in Turkey integrated classroom management as an academic discipline in 1998. However, courses in classroom management are mainly theoretical in nature and inconsequential with regard to practical issues of misbehavior in schools. Moreover, instruction on legal foundations of education is virtually nonexistent in teacher education programs in the country. Most teachers in Turkey ignore students' rights with regard to discipline measures in the classroom. This has the potential for causing serious legal disputes between educators and families concerning the maltreatment of students in schools.

The Turkish education system would greatly benefit from the development and implementation of preservice and in-service teacher education programs in classroom management and legal foundations of education. A knowledgeable teaching force in these subjects would contribute to the modernization of the Turkish classroom which would, in turn, further the social and economic growth and development currently experienced by the country.

KEY POINTS

1. Even though corporal punishment has been banned in Turkish schools since 1923 (law 1702 and state personnel law 657), it is still is prevalent within both the family and school context.
2. In Turkey, approximately 50 percent of children are subjected to different forms and degrees of corporal punishment in schools. Also, most teachers believe in the need of physical punishment as an integral component in the development of the child.
3. Most teacher education programs in Turkey address neither practical issues with regard to classroom management and legal foundations of education, nor practical approaches to the handling of misbehavior in the classroom.
4. The current economic growth and modernization experienced by Turkey must be complemented by the modernization of its educational system and institutions, particularly with regard to practical and legal approaches to discipline in schools.

REFERENCES

Akkok, F., Askar, P., and Sucuoglu, B. (1995, May). "Safe Schools Require the Contributions of Everybody: The Picture in Turkey." *Thresholds in Education*, 29–32.

Atıcı, M., and Merry, R. (2001, June). "Misbehaviour in British and Turkish Primary Classrooms." *Pastoral Care*, 32–39.

Aydın, B. (2010). "Turkish Primary School Pupils' Views on Punishment." *Educational Research and Review* 5(11): 662–67.

Bascı, Z., and Dilekmen, M. (2009). "An Analysis of Classroom Teachers' Attitudes towards Corporal Punishment from the Aspects of Several Variables." *World Applied Sciences Journal* 6(7): 933–38.

Boyacı, A. (2009). Comparative Investigation of Elementary School Students' Opinions about Discipline, Class Rules and Punishment (Turkey-Norway case). *Educational Administration: Theory and Practice* 15(60): 523–53.

Boyraz, A. (2007). *The Discipline Problems which the Teacher Trainees Serving at Primary Schools Encounter*. (Unpublished Master's thesis). Gazi University, Ankara.

Calıskan Maya, I. (2004). "The Teacher Reactions against Undesired Student Behaviours in the Occupational and Technical Schools." Paper presented at XIII National Conference of Educational Sciences, July 6–9, 2004, Inonu University, Malatya, Turkey.

CIA, 2014. *The World Factbook*. Available at: https://www.cia.gov/library/publications/the-world-factbook/geos/tu.html.

Danaoglu, G. (2009). *Student Misbehaviours and Investigating Tackling Strategies of Primary Teachers and Branch Teachers in Fifth Classes of Primary Education*. (Unpublished master's thesis). Cukurova University, Turkey.

Erol, O., Ozaydın, B., and Koc, M. (2010). "Classroom Management Incidents, Teacher Reactions and Effects on Students: A Narrative Analysis of Unforgotten Classroom Memoirs." *Educational Administration: Theory and Practice* 16(1): 25–47.

Gomleksiz, M., et al. (2008). "Schoolyards under the Magnifying Glass: A Qualitative Study on Violence and Children's Rights." *Elementary Education Online* 7(2): 273–87.

Gozutok, D., Er, O., and Karacaoglu, C. (2006). 'Corporal Punishment at School." Paper presented at the International Symposium of Violence and School, March 28–31, 2006, Istanbul, Turkey.

Hatipoglu Sumer, Z., and Aydın, G. (1999). "Incidence of Violence in Turkish Schools: A Review." *International Journal for the Advancement of Counselling* 21, 335–47.

Kilimci, S. (2009). "Teachers' Perceptions on Corporal Punishment as a Method of Discipline in Elementary Schools." *Journal of International Social Research* 2(8), 242–51.

Libal, K. (2001). "Children's Rights in Turkey." *Human Rights Review* Paper 1, 35–44.

OECD. (2005). "Reviews of National Policies for Education: Basic Education in Turkey Background Report." Available at http://www.oecd.org/dataoecd/8/51/39642601.pdf.

OECD. (2011). "Has Discipline in School Deteriorated?" *PISA in Focus* 4. Available at http://www.oecd.org/dataoecd/18/63/47944912.pdf.

Ozben, S. (2010). "Teachers' Strategies to Cope with Student Misbehaviour." *Procedia Social and Behavioral Sciences* 2, 587–94.

Ozkılınc Nezihoğlu, G. and Sabancı, A. (2010). "Views of School Managers about Primary School Students' Misbehaviours and Their Strategies to Cope With." *Pamukkale University, Journal of Education Faculty* (II), 41–53.

PISA (2009). Pisa 2009 results. Available at www.oecd.org/edu/pisa/2009.

SETimes (2011). Turkey country info. Available at http://www.setimes.com/cocoon/setimes/xhtml/en_GB/infoCountryPage/setimes/resource_centre/countries/turkey?country=Turkey.

Sirkeci, B. (2010). *Discipline Problems Encountered during Class Management by Teachers Working in the First Level of the Private and Public Schools and Their Approaches in Handling Discipline Problems*. (Unpublished master's thesis). Fırat University, Turkey.

Siyez, D. M. (2009). "High School Teachers' Perceptions of and Reactions towards the Unwanted Student Behaviours." *Pamukkale University, Journal of Education Faculty* (1): 67–80.

Sumer, Z., and Cetinkaya, E. (2004). "Student, Teacher and Parent Perceptions Regarding Violence in School: A Qualitative Investigation." Paper presented at the European Conference on Educational Research, September 22–25, 2004, University of Crete.

Turkum, A. S. (2010). "Stance against Violence at Schools: School Staff's Ethical Roles in the Well-being of Students in Turkey." *Cultura, International Journal of Philosophy of Culture and Axiology* VII(2): 164–70.

Turnuklu, A., and Galton, M. (2001). "Students' Misbehaviours in Turkish and English Primary Classrooms." *Educational Studies* 27(3): 291–305.

Yazici, S. (2011). "Update: A Guide to Turkish Public Law and Legal Research." Available at http://www.nyulawglobal.org/Globalex/Turkey1.htm#theconstitution.

Yenen, S. (2011). "Turkish Odyssey." Available at http://www.turkishodyssey.com/turkey/turkey.htm.

Chapter Five

Student Discipline from Authoritarian Apartheid to Constitutionalism

South Africa as a Society in Transition

Marius H. Smit and J. P. Rossouw

Student discipline in South Africa is a matter of grave concern.[1] Although national education expenditures have increased[2] while high levels of access to schools and gender parity in the education system have been attained,[3] a large percentage of South African public schools are dysfunctional.[4] Most of these schools are characterized by ineffective management, deficient teaching, and poor student discipline.

The parlous state of student discipline in many South African schools has been attributed to an array of reasons. Most notably among the reasons for poor discipline are the general societal lack of respect for authority, unmotivated and demoralized teachers, regular industrial action in the education sector,[5] their over-politicization by the dominant teachers' union,[6] and incompetence of many officials in the departments of education.[7]

Teachers generally complain that the removal of one of the traditional measures to maintain order and discipline in the form of corporal punishment has left a void in effective disciplinary measures.[8] As a result of these factors the status of teachers has declined in the eyes of their students and the public.[9] What makes the situation worse is that "parents and students have no proper benchmark of what good basic education might entail, and thus they are more accepting of mediocre school and teacher performances and consequently are not fully aware of their predicament."[10]

A ministerial investigation[11] into disadvantaged but resilient schools that provide effective quality education against almost overwhelming odds identified features such as a culture of concern; good governance and community relationships; adequate parental involvement; school safety and good student and educator discipline that these successful schools have in common.

Student discipline in schools can be observed from a variety of perspectives. An educational psychologist might focus on the underlying causes for misconduct, and how to address student behavior through different psychological interventions. Similarly, an education manager might consider different options to put structures and systems in place in an attempt to properly manage student misconduct.

Observed from an Education Law perspective, as in this chapter, consideration is given to the overarching legal system within which schools operate, and in which appropriate disciplinary measures are determined by law. The rest of this chapter then examines the legal framework of education in South Africa and a variety of matters dealing with student discipline in schools, including emerging issues, and a conclusion.

LEGAL FRAMEWORK OF EDUCATION IN SOUTH AFRICA

The primary sources of South African law are legislation, the common law, and case law. The Bill of Rights (chapter 2 of the Constitution) and the South African Schools Act[12] are the main statutory instruments that have a significant bearing on student discipline. Though not always understood or implemented properly, these instruments do in principle provide adequate support and guidance for handling discipline in public schools.

THE BILL OF RIGHTS AND STUDENT DISCIPLINE

The Constitution of South Africa, enacted in 1996, has been widely acclaimed as a model and progressive constitution.[13] The first premise on which the South African legal system is based is section 1(a) of the constitution which provides that South Africa is a constitutional democracy founded on the values of supremacy of the constitution and the rule of law. Constitutional supremacy entails that everybody, including the state, all government institutions, schools, teachers, parents, and students are subject to the constitution.

Concomitant with the doctrine of constitutional supremacy is the concept of the rule of law which entails that the law must apply equally to all and not be arbitrary in the scope of its application.[14] This meaning of the rule of law has developed since it was first described in England[15] and it now includes "a clear set of laws that are freely and easily accessible to all, strong enforcement structures, and an independent judiciary to protect citizens against the arbitrary use of power by the state, individuals or any other organization."[16]

The principle of legality is regarded as the essence of the rule of law and implies that decisions can only be made "by the application of known and general principles of law."[17] Therefore, all endeavors to manage student discipline in South Africa should be based on the premises of constitutional supremacy, the rule of law, and legality.

The three founding values on which the Bill of Rights is based are equality,[18] human dignity,[19] and freedom. The constitution enshrines the right to basic education[20] makes special provision for the right to freedom and security of the person,[21] freedom of religion, belief and opinion,[22] freedom of expression,[23] freedom of association,[24] and the rights of children.[25] Section 28(2) provides that "the best interests of the child is of paramount importance in every matter concerning the child."

LIMITATION OF FUNDAMENTAL HUMAN RIGHTS

Rossouw and De Waal[26] affirm that students often exaggerate their rights by regularly neglecting or ignoring their obligations and by underplaying the corresponding rights of teachers. Wolhuter and Van Staden also found that a tendency to overemphasize students' rights prevails in schools.[27] It is axiomatic that every right has a correlative duty and free societies run the risk of becoming anarchies if individual liberties give rise to general lawlessness and disrespect for the rights of others.[28]

Section 7(3) of the constitution affirms that fundamental human rights are not absolute and are subject to limitations in the Bill of Rights.[29] This limitation of a right is sometimes necessary when the proportional weight and importance accorded to conflicting rights have to be balanced in given circumstances. This is often the case in schools when rights of an ill-disciplined individual have to be weighed against the rights in the form of the security of person and the right to basic education of the law-abiding class of peers, or of specific individuals.

In *Phillips v Manser*[30] the court confirmed the legality of a school governing body's decision to suspend a student from attending the school for serious misconduct pending a decision by the Head of Department (HOD) to expel the student. The student was found guilty of serious misconduct which included assault of another student, dishonestly forging letters, writing graffiti on school furniture, and inhaling chloroform in the science laboratory. The student applied to court to have the governing body's decision reviewed and contended that his right to basic education in terms of section 29(1) of the constitution would be infringed.

The court held that the fundamental right to basic education applies only for the duration of a student's compulsory school age—that is, when a student becomes fifteen years old or finishes grade nine, whichever is the first to occur. It is the duty of the provincial HOD to make other arrangements to accommodate expelled students. The student also contended that the school did not have a code of conduct and that the HOD failed to timely confirm the expulsion within fourteen days of the governing body's recommendation.

J. Kroon of the Eastern Cape High Court ruled in favor of the school, finding that the procedure was fair and the substantive decision was just. The court ruled that the HOD has a limited discretion to decline the recommendation to expel an ill-disciplined student and affirmed that the right to basic education may be limited if students commit serious misconduct. The HOD was therefore obliged to confirm the expulsion.

THE SOUTH AFRICAN SCHOOLS ACT AND STUDENT DISCIPLINE

The purpose of the South African Schools Act is to provide a uniform system for the organization, governance, and funding of schools, and to establish a disciplined and purposeful school environment, dedicated to the maintenance and improvement of quality learning.[31]

The system of school governance enables school governing bodies to take specific regulatory and policy measures to promote an education climate that is conducive to effective teaching and learning. Section 8 of the Schools Act provides that the school governing body must adopt a code of conduct for the students after consultation with the students, parents, and educators of the school, and the code of conduct must be aimed at establishing a disciplined and purposeful school environment, dedicated to the improvement and maintenance of the quality of the learning process.[32]

School rules may not allow for corporal punishment[33] and must prohibit initiation practices.[34] Properly designed rules and policies can go a long way toward establishing safe schools.[35] Well-cared for school facilities, clean and hygienic ablution facilities, functional equipment, well-maintained furniture, and competent personnel create an atmosphere which is conducive to learning and instills a sense of security.

It is well known that unkempt facilities and poorly maintained property encourage vandalism, graffiti, and petty forms of misconduct such as messing with water or littering, simply because it is more difficult to identify and punish the culprit(s).[36] Programmes and measures to address petty misconduct and maintain clean and tidy school environments have led to the reduction of both petty and serious forms of ill-discipline.[37]

COMMON LAW PRINCIPLES AND STUDENT DISCIPLINE

In addition to the legislative framework, the South African legal system rests on various common law principles, which stem from seventeenth-century Roman-Dutch Law and nineteenth-century English law. The constitution recognizes the common law to the extent that it is consistent with the Bill of Rights,[38] but provides that the common law must be developed to promote the spirit, purport, and objects of the Bill of Rights.[39]

The most important common law principles relating to student discipline are the rules of natural justice, which govern due process and just substantive decision making: the *ultra vires*-doctrine and the *in loco parentis* position of the teacher. The common law rules of natural justice have now been codified by the Promotion of Administrative Justice Act.[40] The High Court has jurisdiction to review administrative action and the Constitutional Court is the final court to adjudicate constitutional matters.

The two main components of the rules of natural justice are the rule against bias (*nemo iudex sine causa*: no one may be a judge in his own case); and the *audi alteram partem*-rule (hear the other side). The three elements for a fair hearing are the provision of sufficient and fair notice of the intended hearing; the opportunity to be heard; and the right to representation to assist during the hearing.

A fair hearing requires that adequate notice of the complaints or charges are given and that sufficient time to prepare for the hearing is provided. The *audi*-principle also entails that all parties should be accorded that opportunity for an oral hearing and personal appearance.

In the matter of *Governing Body, Tafelberg School v. Head, Western Cape Education Department*,[41] the governing body of Tafelberg School applied for the review of the decision of the provincial HOD to override the recommendation of school officials that a student who had been found guilty of stealing computer equipment belonging to the school should be expelled.

The HOD's decision was taken in terms of regulation 3(4) of Regulations Relating to Serious Misconduct of Students at Public Schools, under section 9(3) of the Schools Act, which provided that the HOD must decide whether to expel or readmit the pupil after receipt of a report regarding the circumstances leading to the governing body's decision, the minutes of the meeting at which the decision was taken and any written representations of the pupil and his or her parents or representative.

The HOD based his decision to readmit the student only on written submissions made by the student's parents. The school governing body had not been afforded an opportunity to respond to the parents' representations. The court thought that the HOD should have afforded the school a hearing before he had permitted new and further representations from the parents to influence him in his decision. The HOD's decision was set aside and the student was expelled from the school.

THE STATE OF STUDENT MISCONDUCT IN SCHOOLS

The stark reality regarding the current South African education sphere is that the system is under pressure, partly dysfunctional on various levels, and severely unionized, which inevitably results in poor academic results.

Frequency and Forms of Student Misconduct in South African Schools

In a series of empirical studies over the past decade, which were inter alia conducted in at schools in five provinces[42] of South Africa, Oosthuizen found that ordinary forms of misconduct such as dereliction of duties, untidiness, dishonesty occur almost on a daily basis and that medium and serious misconduct occur less frequently. Table 5.1 ranks the types of student misconduct according to the frequency of occurrence in most South African schools.

What is disturbing from this empirical data is the misconduct such as use of foul language is the second most frequent infringement and that disrespect toward teachers, theft, violence, and vandalism occur on a monthly basis in most schools in South Africa.

Teachers, school principals, and governing bodies have to cope with two basic problems in this regard, which both impact on the effectiveness of the teaching process:

- a series of ongoing, less serious forms of general misconduct, ranging from students not doing their tasks, unruly talking, remarks and disruptiveness preventing teachers to use the available teaching time optimally.
- intermittent incidences of different forms of serious misconduct, often criminal in nature.

School-based Violence

One aspect of the right to basic education includes the rights of students and educators to learn and teach in a safe environment, free from all forms of violence and schools, and the state has a duty to provide a safe environment that supports and promotes children's dignity and development.[43] However, it is very disturbing that the environment and climate necessary for effective teaching and learning in South Africa has been increasingly undermined by a culture of school-based violence.

Table 5.1. Forms and Frequency of Student Misconduct in South African Schools.

MISCONDUCT	RANKING Most to least frequent	FREQUENCY
Dereliction of duties	1	±1 x week
Swearing and foul language	2	±1 x week
Untidiness	3	±1 x week
Dishonesty and telling lies	4	±1 x week
Absence without permission	5	±1 x week
Laziness and poor attitude	6	±1 x week
Bullying	7	±1 x week
Disruption of the class/lesson	8	±1 x week
Rudeness and talking back	9	±1 x month
Moodiness and aggressiveness	10	±1 x month
Disrespect towards educators	11	±1 x month
Theft	12	±1 x month
Violence	13	±1 x month
Vandalism	14	±1 x month
Crimen iniuria and defamation	15	±1 x year
Graffiti	16	±1 x year
Smoking	17	±1 x year
Gang activities	18	≤ 1 x year
Alcohol abuse	19	≤ 1 x year
Sexual harassment	20	≤ 1 x year
Drug abuse	21	≤ 1 x year
Pornography	22	≤ 1 x year

Source: Oosthuizen (2006):3–4.

Manifestations of School-based Violence

The right to basic education is infringed if it takes place in an environment that is not free from violence.[44] A study by the South African Human Rights Commission in 2008 confirmed that violence in many South African schools has reached alarming proportions.[45]

Manifestations of school-based violence is multidimensional and often depends on the context in which it arises, such as whether the violence is perpetrated by students against fellow students, by educators against students, by students against educators or by external persons against both students and educators.

Bullying, gender-based violence, accidental violence, discrimination and violence, sexual violence and harassment, physical violence and psychological violence, describe some of the most prevalent forms identified by the Human Rights Commission in 2008. Students now seem more willing and able to employ physically aggressive methods by using knives, weapons, and handguns more readily used than before.[46]

Freedom and Security of Person

The essence of Education Law is the security, safety, wellness, and general welfare (*geborgenheit*) of students, educators, and other parties at schools.[47] Numerous provisions in the constitution protect the rights of students and teachers to learn and teach in a safe environment which is free from all forms of violence.

Students have the right to, among others: an environment free from racial and gender discrimination (section 9(3)); human dignity (section 10); life (section 11); freedom and security of person (section 12);[48] protection from maltreatment, neglect, and abuse or degradation (section 28(d); and basic education (section 29). Section 12 of the constitution has a direct bearing on student safety and security at schools and provides that everyone has the right to be free from all forms of violence from either public or private sources. Section 12(1)(c–e) reiterates that disciplinary measures must be free of all forms of violence and that students may not be treated or punished in cruel, inhuman, or degrading ways.

Assault and Common Crime

The National Youth Victimisation Study, as quoted by the Human Rights Commission,[49] interviewed more than 4,500 young people aged between the ages of twelve and twenty-two nationally. Just over two-fifths (41.4 percent) of the young people interviewed had been victims of some form of crime in the year preceding the study.

The most common crime experienced was theft of personal property while assault constituted the second most common crime, with 16.5 percent of the young people being assaulted in the twelve-month period under review. One-tenth (9.4 percent) of those interviewed had been victims of robbery. Both these crimes are classified as violent and usually result in injuries to the person. Another 4.2 percent of interviewees were victims of sexual assault.

Bullying

Bullying is frequently associated with discrimination against students from poor families, racially marginalized groups, or those with particular personal characteristics (e.g., appearance, or a physical or mental disability).[50] Bullying[51] is most commonly verbal, but physical harassment may also occur. Schools are also affected by events in the wider community, such as the prevalence of gang culture, gang-related criminal activity, and the use and abuse of drugs.

Sexual and gender-based violence also occurs in educational settings with most incidences targeted against girls by male educators and classmates. There are increased reports of violence being targeted against lesbian, gay, bisexual, and transgendered young people. Psychological violence is an umbrella term that encompasses bullying, harassment, victimization, abusive threats, and intimidation.

Violence by Students against Educators

The prevalence of violence by students against educators is not very high. Still, incidences do occur. The teachers' unions complain that teachers experience physical assaults; incidences of psychological violence; students acting disrespectfully; students swearing at and taunting educators; students disrupting classes; and students bullying educators.

Jacobs v. Chairman, Governing Body, Rhodes High School[52] dramatically illustrates the terrible results of school-based violence where a thirteen-year-old student violently attacked a teacher by repeatedly hitting her with a hammer. Having suffered multiple injuries to the skull and fractured bones, the teacher is no longer able to work, claimed damages, and was awarded an amount of R3 250,000 as compensation.

The student was expelled and sent to an industrial school. The court found the principal and other staff members were negligent and held the state liable in terms of section 60 of the Schools Act. Although matters such as *Jacobs* are usually dealt with in terms of the law of delict and criminal law, the victim's fundamental right to freedom and security of person is also infringed by such acts of violence.

Negative Consequences of School Violence for Students

The right to basic education ought to be available, accessible, acceptable, and adaptable,[53] but the state has thus far not adequately honored this obligation. The reasons for this is, first, because the quality of the education in most public schools is deficient and, second, because a large percentage (33.3 percent) of students drop out of the system for reasons not always linked to their own competence or potential.[54]

The most disappointing and far reaching setback of postapartheid South Africa, thus far, has been the dismally poor scholastic results of the education system.[55] Absent a culture of teaching and learning,[56] as reflected by the country's poor academic performance, student misconduct thrives.

School violence can lead to serious consequences including suicide;[57] numeracy and literacy learning problems; limited concentration span; poor performance in class; high absentee and dropout rates; being unmotivated in class; and in general, loss of desire to succeed in life. It is therefore essential to root out all forms of school violence in South Africa.

PROHIBITION OF CORPORAL PUNISHMENT: A CAUSE OF ILL-DISCIPLINE?

Teachers feel disempowered in the human rights environment because one of the traditional measures to maintain order and discipline, corporal punishment, has been abolished.[58] Since 1996 the Schools Act prohibits all forms of corporal punishment,[59] depicting it as "an offence and liable on conviction to a sentence which could be imposed for assault."

Over the past fifteen years some of the effects of this general ban on corporal punishment in schools have become apparent. Student discipline has become a serious problem in South African schools. As a result, many teachers blame the parlous state of poor discipline in many schools on the fact that educators no longer have an effective deterrent as a form of punishment.

The majority of teachers (58 percent) favor the reinstatement of corporal punishment in schools and many admit to the continued use of corporal punishment to instill discipline in schools.[60] Wolhuter and Van Staden[61] found that 85 percent of teachers are of the view that student discipline problems make them unhappy in their work, and 79 percent have at times considered quitting the teaching profession because of student discipline problems.

Nevertheless, the Constitutional Court held in the matter of *Christian Education South Africa v Minister of Education*[62] that corporal punishment is a form of cruel and degrading punishment that violates a person's human dignity and thus infringes section 12(1)(e) of the Constitution. The prohibition of corporal punishment at schools was thus declared constitutional. J. Sachs explained the reason for the prohibition of corporal punishment at schools as follows: "It had a principled and symbolic function, manifestly intended to promote respect for the dignity and physical and emotional integrity of all children."

The court held that religious views that allow for corporal punishment may be justifiably limited in terms of section 36 of the constitution. Although corporal punishment is prohibited at schools, the reasonable and moderate use of corporal punishment by parents at places other than schools remains lawful and has not been prohibited in terms of South African law.

Despite the prohibition, a number of studies indicate that teachers still apply corporal punishment at schools. The Human Rights Commission reported[63] that corporal punishment is still applied in more than half of the schools (51.4 percent), with the Eastern Cape (65.3 percent), Mpumalanga (64.1 percent), and Limpopo (55.7 percent) reporting the highest incidences. The report indicates that that 58 percent of educators are in favor of the reinstatement of corporal punishment, while 28 percent conceded to still using corporal punishment.

In the matter of *George v. Member of the Executive Council, Eastern Cape Education Department*,[64] the plaintiff instituted an action claiming damages in his personal capacity, and as father and natural guardian of his minor son. The claim arose from an alleged assault of the boy by a teacher in the form of corporal punishment when he was caned by his teacher.

The Education Department admitted that the teacher acted as an employee in the course of his employment when the incident occurred but denied vicarious liability as the teacher had not acted in accordance with the terms and conditions of employment. On that specific day, on returning to class after break, the teacher found that the cabinet where administrative files and books for students were stored had been vandalized, and that the contents were strewn all over the classroom floor.

The two culprits were identified and the teacher meted out six lashes on the buttocks of each boy as punishment. The one boy's wrist was fractured when he tried to block one of the lashes. The court held the Education Department vicariously liable for damages for its employee's conduct.

Teachers that contravene the law by applying corporal punishment run the risk of facing criminal charges for assault, civil action for damages, and being disciplined by the employer.[65] In addition, such teachers may have their professional license to teach revoked by the South African Council of Educators.

TEACHER MISCONDUCT: A FACTOR INFLUENCING STUDENT BEHAVIOR

One prominent reason for student misconduct from within the education system is the conduct and poor example set by a large contingent of teachers. While there are many diligent and law-abiding teachers that provide excellent teaching, where an average pass rate of 96 percent is maintained, in approximately 20 percent of the public schools, the majority of teachers are influenced by activist or highly politicized unions such as the South African Democratic Teacher's Union.[66]

Some union leaders and departmental officials tend to advance their own political agendas and thus ignore the ethical and democratic values on which the Constitution is based.[67] Affiliated with the Council for South African Trade Unions, the majority of members of this union do not view education as a profession and teachers are regarded as mere workers. The result is annual strikes, characterized by intimidation, violence, and vandalism.

Students observe such negative examples and are obviously influenced by the general lawless conduct of teachers. Within such a society and education system, where leaders and teachers regularly defy the rule of law, it is understandable that the youth will also commit forms of serious misconduct.

METHODS OF DEALING WITH STUDENT MISCONDUCT

In view of the prohibition of corporal punishment, Oosthuizen set out to find alternative best practices and determine the most effective means of dealing with student misconduct in schools. Perhaps it should not come as a surprise that Oosthuizen found in his series of empirical studies that the most effective method is proper preparation by the teacher and the first ten best practices are by and large dependent on the preparedness, competence, and attitude of the teacher (see table 5.2).

The participants in the quantitative empirical studies of Oosthuizen involved teachers from five provinces in South Africa and the results indicate the methods that work best according to the teachers. The ranking of measures from most to least effective dealing with student ill-discipline and to ensure a disciplined school environment are listed in table 5.2.

It is interesting to note that the preventative approach and an emphasis on self-discipline and good values reap the most benefits.[68] Although the participants affirmed that reactive methods such as meetings with or phoning the parents, disciplinary hearings, and punishments (e.g., detention, isolation in class, community service, and chores) are necessary from time to time to deal with serious misconduct, the most energy and time efficient approach is to focus on preventative measures and to prepare and teach properly.[69] Teachers that come ill-prepared, have poor subject knowledge, or are lazy to do their duty tend to have more frequent and serious student discipline problems.[70]

School Policy and Regulatory Measures to Improve Safety and Discipline

The system of school governance enables school governing bodies to take specific regulatory and policy measures to improve the safety and well-being at schools. The legal measures include the following:

- to adopt a Code of Conduct (section 8 & section 20(1)(d));

Table 5.2 Ranking Methods of Maintaining Discipline

Ranking Most to Least Effective	Method of Discipline
1	Proper preparation by teacher
2	Good subject knowledge by teacher
3	Positive discipline measures
4	Meeting/discussion with parents
5	System of classroom rules
6	Rewards and awards
7	Emphasis on values
8	Encouraging pride /self-respect
9	Reference to school principal
10	Regular prayers by teachers
11	Student participation in drafting code of conduct
12	Reprimand
13	Extra work/chores
14	Encourage traditions
15	Merit-demerit system
16	Removal of privileges
17	Disciplinary hearing
18	Community service
19	Detention
20	Isolation in classroom
21	Isolation outside classroom
22	Corporal punishment

Source: Oosthuizen (2006):24.

- to conduct disciplinary hearings before suspending or recommending expulsion of ill-disciplined students (section 9);
- to determine the times of the school day (section 20(1)(f));
- to administer and control the school's property, buildings and grounds which are occupied by the school (section 20(1)(g);
- to determine regulations and procedures for search and seizure;[71]
- to recommend the appointment of educators at a school to the HOD (section 20(i)); and
- to recommend the appointment of non-educator staff at the school to the HOD (section 20(j)).

Even though these measures do not, at first glance, seem to address school safety directly, every one of these measures contributes to the creation of an orderly, secure, respectful school culture and environment.

Dealing with Serious Misconduct: Suspension and Expulsion of Students

The ultimate means available to school official in dealing with serious student misconduct is to suspend offenders for seven days or to recommend expulsion from the school in terms of section 9 of the Schools Act. School governing bodies must conduct fair disciplinary hearings before suspending learners. Such disciplinary hearings are intimidating and unpleasant experiences that most students usually want to avoid.

In terms of section 9(1) of the Schools Act, governing bodies may, on reasonable grounds and as precautionary measures, suspend students immediately to ensure school safety and avoid further violence or damage after students have been granted reasonable opportunities to make representations (during an informal enquiry) in relation to their suspension. If expulsions from the school are the findings, governing bodies must make recommendations to HODs who have the final say in the matters. HODs have a qualified discretion to refuse the recommendation of expulsions.

Reasonableness in terms of section 33(1) of the constitution implies decisions that are "structured" in a rational fashion.[72] This means that orders must be supported by the evidence and information before administrators and the reasons given for acting. Reasonableness also implies reasonable effects, also known as proportionality.[73]

The principle of ensuring fair procedure ("due process") and substantively correct decisions is illustrated by the matter of *Van Biljon v. Crawford*,[74] in which two students were dishonest during an examination and illegally used "crib notes." The students were caught red-handed by the invigilator. During an informal hearing or enquiry that was held in the principal's office, the students were given the opportunity to make representations and admitted the misconduct. The students were punished and Van Biljon was demoted and lost his badge as a student representative (leader).

One of the students contested the procedural fairness of the informal hearing and denied guilt in the matter. It was argued that the hearing had not complied with the education department's guidelines for a fair disciplinary hearing. The court upheld the precedent set in *Shidiak v. Union Government 1912 AD*, which provides that if an official (such as the principal *in casu*) is charged with a duty and exercises his discretionary competency by applying his mind and deciding in good faith—that is, *bona fide* not *mala fide*, then the court is not entitled to replace the official's decision by its own.

The court also found that the procedure followed during the informal hearing did not have to comply strictly with the guidelines for section 9 of the Schools Act, because the punishment did not involve suspension or expulsion from a school. The court will defer to the principals if they exercise their discretionary competencies reasonably and in good faith.

Therefore, *Van Biljon* confirms that as long as it is procedurally fair and the decision is substantively just, then an informal hearing may be conducted at a school on matters not leading to suspensions or expulsions.

If a crime has been committed, a criminal charge may be laid against a student by either the complainant or an educator, the school, or a member of the governing body of a school. Whenever minors are charged with criminal offences, the senior public prosecutor and the probation officer of the local magistrate's court play key roles in dealing with the issue.

The standard procedure is for all criminal matters involving minors to be postponed indefinitely by the court to give the accused minor the opportunity to undergo rehabilitation by means of the so-called diversion process. This entails that the probation officer follows the following steps:

- The teacher or the principal or the governing body lays the charge with an identified investigating officer (policeman) at the police station.
- Should the transgressor be younger than eighteen years of age, the probation officer has to be notified within twenty-four hours.
- The probation officer then sets in motion a youth rehabilitation program.
- The purpose of this program is *diversion from the criminal courts* to prevent a recurrence of such offences and to avoid incarceration of minors.

The diversion process is a rehabilitative one based on the principles of restorative justice. It is an inherently fair process to restore justice to victims and an equally effective mechanism to address criminal tendencies with youth offenders. The deterrent effect of the diversion process has been found to be very successful in preventing recurrence of serious forms of misconduct.[75]

Unwillingness of Education Officials to Expel Ill-Disciplined Students

A problem regularly encountered by schools in disciplinary matters that involve expulsion is unreasonable delay to reach a decision by HODs. This reluctance on the side of officials to expel ill-disciplined students has given rise to litigation by frustrated schools.

In *Maritzburg College v. Dlamini NO and Others*,[76] three students were found guilty during October 2003, after a procedurally correct investigation and hearing, of smashing the window of a hired bus. Two of them were found to be smelling of alcohol and a bottle of brandy was discovered in one student's sports bag. Apparently all three of the students had, in the past, been guilty of frequent acts of misbehavior.

After recommending expulsion, school officials waited unreasonably long for a response to their recommendation. During the eventual hearing an official pointed out that they previously had to wait on three different occasions for between a year and twenty-one months for the first respondent, the HOD, to react to their repeated correspondence.

The HOD said it was "utterly unreasonable" to expect him to make a decision within two months. In this case the reaction only came after he was summoned to a High Court hearing. The judge frowned on the unwillingness of the HOD to make an expeditious decision and declared that "consideration must be given in future, in my view, where litigants are forced to come to court to compel public servants to carry out their duties where they have failed to do so, that such officials be ordered to pay the costs incurred, personally."

These cases illustrate the frustration of schools and the very unsatisfactory results for schools. Such obstructionist attitudes of departmental officials break down the authority of governing bodies and principals. The present provisions of the South African Schools Act place an unfair burden on schools that, in practice, have no other effective means of dealing with serious misconduct. A more effective remedy would be to amend section 9 of the Schools Act to allow for lengthy suspension of up to 180 days (i.e., one academic year).

EMERGING ISSUES

The Right to Privacy and Student Discipline

The right to privacy is recognized in common law and after the promulgation of the Constitution in 1996 it was elevated as a fundamental right. The courts[77] have in the past ruled that a person's right to privacy was invaded when, for example, the person's photo was published in an advertisement without consent; where a dentist informed another person about the HIV status of one of his patients; by wire-tapping the conversations of a private person and by peeping at a person who was getting undressed. Questions that arise with regard to the right to privacy in schools are:

- How far do students' rights to privacy extend at school?
- May the possessions of students be searched for illegal substances or dangerous weapons?
- May students who have such objects with them at school be searched?
- May these objects be confiscated by the teacher?

- What about the safety of the other students at school?

In the matter of *De Reuck v. Director of Public Prosecutions*[78] the Constitutional Court referred to the concept of "spheres of privacy" which entails the notion that there is an inverse correlation between the strength of the privacy right and the sphere of conduct. The right to privacy is strongest in a person's inner sanctum which is usually the bedroom, bathroom, and exclusive areas of a private dwelling and weaker in public spheres of operation. Applying this principle to schools, the possession of dangerous weapons or drugs would entitle the school to limit the right to privacy of students by searching their private possessions and seizing the contraband to prevent harm to others.

The 2001 Regulations for Safety Measures at Public Schools[79] contain extensive provisions authorizing a HOD or principal to prohibit violent or dangerous activities at public schools. All public schools have been declared violence- and drug-free zones. No person may enter a school premises or allow, use, possess, carry, or store any dangerous object, alcohol, or illegal drugs at the school. This provision applies to extracurricular activities such as school tours, camping or cultural excursions, and sporting events as well.[80]

Police officials and school principals or their delegates are authorized to search any public school premises without a warrant, provided that a reasonable suspicion of unauthorized activity exists.[81] Contraband may be seized without a warrant, to ensure the safety of the public school.[82] The requirements for valid searches are:[83]

- The purpose of the search must be to act on credible information that leads to reasonable suspicion.
- The place where the search is done should not unfairly or unreasonably infringe on the student's right to privacy and dignity.
- The person conducting the search must have the authority to do so.
- The manner in which the search is conducted must be legally correct.
- Boys and girls should be separated and searched by a person of the same gender.

Importantly, these regulations do not allow for suspicionless searches such as random spot-checks. Whether sufficient evidence exists to form a reasonable suspicion would depend on the facts and circumstances of each specific case and whether a reasonable person would believe a good reason from a credible source exists, then the search and subsequent seizure would be valid.[84]

Freedom of Expression and Discipline in Schools

Section 16 of the South African Constitution protects the broader concept "freedom of expression" and not only freedom of speech, which is the standard term used in America. Freedom of expression extends to include all forms of verbal or nonverbal acts by which a person conveys an idea, emotion, belief, or grievance.[85]

Section 16 protects free expression generally, which includes the freedom of the press and media, the freedom to impart information and ideas, and academic and artistic freedom, but prohibits propaganda for war; enticement of imminent violence; or advocacy of hatred that is based on race, ethnicity, gender, or religion that constitutes incitement to cause imminent harm. In the matter of *Afriforum v. Malema*,[86] the High Court held that the true yardstick of hate speech is neither the historical significance nor the context in which the words were uttered, but the effect of the words, objectively considered, on those directly affected and targeted thereby.

Religious Expression Contravening School Dress Codes

Van Vollenhoven explains that during the apartheid era the majority of South African citizens were denied the right to speak out against the government and in schools even the students were prevented from questioning teachers or authorities.[87] The result was that in the authoritarian political climate of Apartheid, students were not encouraged to think critically and were taught to accept authority without question.

In the multicultural, multilingual, and multireligious context of South African schools freedom of expression issues such as wearing religious clothing and hairstyles, beards, or body piercing or markings in breach of a school's uniform dress code may be relevant for the maintenance of school discipline.

In *Antonie v. Governing Body, the Settlers High School*,[88] the School Governing Body suspended a student from school for wearing dreadlocks in contravention of the school's uniform dress code. The student was a Rastafarian who wore the dreadlocks under a cap as part of her religious practice.

J. Van Zyl of the High Court held that the infringement of the school's uniform dress code was not a serious misconduct and did not warrant suspension. The student's dreadlocks had not caused a substantial disruption of school discipline and did not prevent others from receiving education. The suspension was set aside.

Freedom of Expression and Unfair Discrimination Based on Culture

In *MEC for Education, Kwazulu-Natal v. Pillay*,[89] a mother applied on behalf of her daughter, a student at Durban Girls High public school, to wear a gold nose-stud to school, in keeping with her South Indian family traditions and Hindu culture. Officials refused exemption from the code of conduct on the ground that wearing of a nose-stud would impact negatively on school discipline of the school. Officials feared that similar exemptions from the school's code of conduct would impact negatively on discipline at the school.

The matter eventually went to the Constitutional Court where the student contended that her right to freedom of expression had been unjustifiably limited because the nose-stud posed no risk of substantial disruption to school activities. School officials presented no evidence to show that a student who was granted an exemption from the uniform dress code would be any less disciplined or that it would negatively affect the discipline of others. The court held that allowing the exemption to wear the stud would not impose too great a burden on the school.

The Constitutional Court also found that the norm embodied by the school's code was not neutral, but that it enforced mainstream and historically privileged forms of adornment, such as earrings which involve the piercing of a body part in Western culture, at the expense of an Asiatic minority and historically excluded forms.[90] The court held that the code of conduct, coupled with the decision to refuse the student an exemption, amounted to unfair discrimination which unconstitutionally limited her right to express her religion and culture.

Freedom of Expression Does Not Equate to a Right to Be Ill-Disciplined

In *Western Cape Residents' Association obo Williams v. Parow High School*,[91] the parents of a student in grade twelve applied for an urgent interdict to compel officials to allow her daughter to attend the matric farewell function. The school had refused the student permission as a result of her continued ill-discipline during the course of the year.

In casu there was not legislation or a common law rule that determined whether the student had a right against the school to attend the matric farewell function. In determining whether a rule should be developed to give effect to the constitution, the court considered the arguments that the student's dignity, equality, and freedom of expression had been infringed by the school's refusal.

However, the court found that the attendance of a matric farewell function is a social activity and, as such, was a privilege and not an enforceable right. Also, the court considered the interests of school officials, other students, and the applicant in deciding on balance that:

> Two of the important lessons that a school must teach its students are discipline and respect for authority. The granting of privilege as a reward for good

> behaviour is one tool that may be used to teach such lessons. The withholding of such privilege can therefore not be claimed as an infringement of a right to equality or to dignity. . . . The right to freedom of expression, of course, does not equate to a right to be ill-disciplined or rude. The system of rewards for good behaviour permeates all walks of life and to learn the system at an early age can only benefit the student later on in his or her life.[92]

Defamation, Cyber-Bullying, and Freedom of Expression

In *Le Roux v Dey*[93] schoolchildren had published a computer-created image in which the face of the deputy principal of their school was super-imposed alongside that of the school principal on an image of two naked men sitting in a sexually suggestive posture. The school crests were superimposed over the genital areas of the two men. The deputy principal instituted action and claimed damages for defamation.

As background it is important to note that an action for defamation is aimed at compensating the victim for any publication that injures the plaintiff in his good name and reputation. Its focus is the protection of the constitutional rights to dignity and privacy of any person. When a court assesses whether a publication is defamatory through the prism of the constitution, it is concerned with the interpretation, protection, and enforcement of the constitution.

This case involved the balancing of the rights to dignity and privacy on the one hand, with freedom of expression, and the rights of children on the other. The Freedom of Expression Institute (first *amicus curiae*) argued that the right to freedom of expression included the rights of children to freedom of satirical expression. Having regard to South Africa's recent past of thought control, censorship, and enforced conformity to governmental theories, the court emphasized that the free and open exchange of ideas is no less important than it is in the United States.

On the merits, the applicants (schoolboys) contended that to regard the picture as defamatory would be to lose touch with the ways of schoolchildren and schoolboy pranks. J. Brand, on behalf of the majority of the Constitutional Court, considered whether the humor of the manipulated image was excusable, but held that a jest is not legitimate, if the joke would be insulting, offensive, or degrading to another.

The court held that the question is not so much whether the attempt at a joke is objectively funny or not. Nor is it of any real consequence whether we regard the joke as unsavory or not. A statement which raises a laugh is defamatory when there is an element of *contumelia* in the joke, that is, when it is insulting or degrading to the butt of the joke.

The real question was whether the reasonable observer—perhaps, while laughing—will understand the joke as belittling the plaintiff; as making the plaintiff look foolish and unworthy of respect; or as exposing the plaintiff to ridicule and contempt. If the joke then achieves that purpose, it is defamatory, even when it is hilariously funny to everyone, apart from the victim. The test was thus whether it is a joke in which the subject cannot share because it is hurtful and defamatory to the subject. The court thus confirmed that the publication of the manipulated photograph was not only contrary to common law but also to the constitution and ordered compensation to be paid to the plaintiff.

CONCLUSION

The constitutional standards and fundamental rights support the maintenance of student discipline in South African schools. Also, the Schools Act contains numerous provisions to enhance student discipline. Only the prohibition of corporal punishment at schools has hampered the maintenance of student discipline to some extent. Teachers feel disempowered by the prohibition of corporal punishment and several studies confirm the continued application of corporal punishment in South African schools.

However, not only does the fundamental right to freedom and security of person protect an individual against public violence by the state, but it also protects every person's physical and psychological integrity against private violence. Schools should by definition be safe places where students are able to learn in a disciplined and purposeful environment. In this regard, the nature and extent of poor discipline and school-based violence in many South African schools is a grave cause for concern.

Phillips affirmed that the right to basic education is not absolute and that learners who commit serious misconduct may justifiably be expelled to maintain orderly and disciplined learning environments. The examples of *Tafelberg*, *Pearson*, *Maritzburg College*, and *George Randell* provide substantiation for the fact that at times officials struggle about whether to expel students as a result of administrative injustice and obstructionist attitudes of the education authorities.

At present, the provisions of the Schools Act place an unfair burden on schools that, in practice, have no other effective means of dealing with serious misconduct. A week's suspension is ineffectual, because learners usually regard it as a "holiday" or welcome rest from school obligations. This undermines the design of the Schools Act that is aimed at promoting a disciplined school environment.

The South African courts have endorsed the importance and value of freedom of expression in a democracy and that the Constitution recognizes that individuals need to be able to hear, form, and express opinions and views freely on a wide range of matters. In cases where freedom of expression can be reasonably accommodated at a school without the likelihood of substantive disruption of school discipline, the school should tolerate the cultural and religious expression by allowing for exemptions from the school rules.

When not threatening school discipline, the South African courts have ruled in favor of upholding students' right to freedom of expression. On the other hand, when expressions are untrue or cause harm to people, then the courts have not hesitated to declare such defamatory statements, images, or forms of hate-speech unlawful and unconstitutional.

In sum, the available policy, constitutional, regulatory, and administrative measures are sufficient to ensure the establishment of a purposeful learning environment in South African schools. However, it is imperative that these measures should be appropriately implemented and, second, that teachers should set proper examples and comply with their duties as competent professionals by preparing properly, having good subject knowledge and by focusing on the preventative approach to maintain student discipline in the classroom.

KEY POINTS

1. The most effective method of ensuring a disciplined classroom is proper preparation and adequate subject knowledge by the teacher.
2. Unlawful conduct by teachers and systemic dysfunctionality undermines the culture of learning and contributes to school-based violence.
3. Constitutionalism and enshrined fundamental rights enable a safe and disciplined school environment.
4. Freedom of expression should be accommodated in schools insofar as it does not result in substantive disruption of discipline.
5. Harmful expressions of ideas, even if humorous, are unlawful if the victims feel that their dignity has been infringed.
6. Appropriate legislative provisions should be enacted to enable schools and administrators to deal effectively with serious misconduct by students.

NOTES

1. Wolhuter, C. C., Oosthuizen, I. J., and Van Staden, J. G. (2010). Skoolfase/Leerderouderdom as Faktor in Leerderdissipline in Suid-Afrikaanse Skole. *Tydskrif vir Christelike Wetenskap* 40(1): 169–86.

2. Department of Education. (2007). Presentation to select committees of Finance, Social Services, Education and Recreation. In real terms the spending on the average public ordinary school student is 30 percent higher in 2007 than it was in 1994.

3. Department of Education. (2009). Annual Report for 2009 at 14.

4. Taylor, G. (2006). Focus on: challenges across the education spectrum. JET Bulletin, (15):1–9. According to most studies approximately 80 percent of the schools are by and large dysfunctional and the quality of the education is deficient.

5. Du Plessis, T. (2010). Staking: Hofbevele gekry teen dié wat intimideer. Naweek-Beeld: August 21.

6. Zille, H. (2010). On the teachers' right to strike. Extract from speech delivered by the DA Leader at the Suid-Afrikaanse Onderwysersunie Principals' Symposium in Port Elizabeth. Issued by the Democratic Alliance, August 31.

7. Colditz, P. (2011). Principles for a new legislative framework to improve school education in South Africa. Paper presented at the 16th annual international conference of the SA Education Law Association. Umhlanga Rocks. September 21.

8. Section 10 of the South African Schools Act prohibits corporal punishment by anyone at a school.

9. Smit, M. H. (2009). A model for improving democratic school governance in South Africa-An Education Law Perspective. PhD thesis, North-West University.

10. Motala, S., and Dieltiens, V. (2010). Educational Access in South Africa: Country Research Summary. Consortium for Research on Educational Access, Transitions and Equity University of the Witwatersrand, 10. Education Polity Unit (EPU). Accessed on April 17, 2012, available at: http://www.create-upc.org/pdf_documents/ South_Africa_Country_Research_Summary.pdf.

11. Department of Education. (2008). Ministerial Report: Schools that work at 5.

12. Act 84 of 1996.

13. Sunstein, C. R. (2001). Social and economic rights? Lessons from South Africa. Univ. of Chicago Public Law and Legal Theory, Working Paper No. 12.

14. Cheadle, H., Davis, D., and Haysom, C. (2006). *South African Constitutional Law: The Bill of Rights*, 30–38.

15. Currie, I., and De Waal, J. (2010). The Bill of Rights Handbook. 5th ed. Claremont: Juta at 10.

16. Viljoen, T. (2014). There can be no Rule of Law unless there is access to the basic sources of law. Accessed on April 28, 2014, available at http://www.lexisnexis.co.za/about-us/rule-of-law/transparency.aspx.

17. Currie and De Waal (n 15 at 11).

18. Section 9.

19. Section 10.

20. Section 29(1)(a) "Everyone has the right to a basic education, including adult basic education."

21. Section 12.

22. Section 15.

23. Section 16.

24. Section 18.

25. Section 28.

26. Rossouw, J. P., and De Waal, E. (2003). Who minds the educators while the students are on strike? Paper presented at the 8th annual international conference of the SA Education Law Association. Magoebaskloof. 10 September.

27. Wolhuter, C. C., and Van Staden, J. G. (2007). Student misconduct in the Free State, Eastern Cape and Vaal Triangle (South Africa): an empirical study of the experiences of teachers. In Oosthuizen, I. J., et al. (Eds.). 2007. Perspectives on student conduct: Proceedings of the International Conference on Student Discipline, April 2–4, Potchefstroom, South Africa. at 394–405.

28. Smit, M. H. (ed.). (2013). Fundamentals of Human Rights and Democracy in Education—A South African perspective. Van Schaik: Pretoria at 6.

29. *De Reuck v Director of Public Prosecution.* (2004) (1) SA 406 (CC) para 89B. Fundamental rights may be limited in the following ways: Limitation in terms of the general limitation provision; definitional demarcation of a right; Specific limitations of a right; or suspension of rights during a state of emergency as regulated by section 37 of the Constitution.

30. *Phillips v Manser* [1999] 1 All SA 198 (SE).

31. Schools Act—Long title: "To provide for a uniform system for the organisation, governance and funding of schools; to amend and repeal certain laws relating to schools; and to provide for matters connected therewith." Section 8(2) provides that a school's code of conduct

"must be aimed at establishing a disciplined and purposeful school environment, dedicated to the improvement and maintenance of the quality of the learning process."

32. Department of Education. (1998). Guidelines for the consideration of Governing Bodies in adopting a Code of Conduct for Students. *Government Gazette* vol. 395, no. 18900, May 15, 1998. General notice, Department of Education, Notice 776 of 1998.
33. Section 10.
34. Section 10A.
35. Oosthuizen, I. J. (ed.) (2008). Safe schools. Center for Education Law and Policy: Pretoria at 83–84.
36. Wilson, J. Q., and Kelling, G. L. (1997). Broken Windows. In: Dunham RG and Alpert GP (eds.) *Critical Issues in Policing: Contemporary Readings;* Also: Wagers ML Broken Windows Policing: The LAPD experience. PhD thesis. State University of New Jersey. 'Broken windows' policing has been credited with the historic successes in crime reduction in New York, Los Angeles and schools in America.
37. Oosthuizen, I. J. (ed.). (2010). A practical guide to discipline in schools. Van Schaik: Pretoria at 70.
38. Section 39(3).
39. Section 39(2).
40. 3 of 2000. South Africa (Republic) 2000.
41. 2000 (1) SA 1209 (C).
42. The provinces of Western Cape, Eastern Cape, Northern Cape, Free State and North-West.
43. South African Human Rights Commission (SAHRC)(2008). Report on school-based violence at 1.
44. SAHRC (n 43 at 5).
45. Ibid.
46. SAHRC (n 43 at 9).
47. Oosthuizen, I. J. (2010). *Aspects of Education Law*, Van Schaik: Pretoria at 1–10.
48. Section 12 of the Constitution.
49. SAHRC (n 45 at 10).
50. SAHRC (n 47 at 11).
51. Coloroso, B. (2009). *The Bully, the Bullied, and the Bystander*. Bullying is defined as physical, verbal or psychological aggression that occurs repeatedly and is marked by an imbalance of power, intent to harm, threat of further aggression, and the creation of terror in the victim.
52. *Jacobs v Chairman, Governing Body, Rhodes High School* (2011) (1) SA 160 (WCC).
53. Tomasevski, K. (2001). Right to Education Primers No 3 Human Rights obligations: making education available, accessible, acceptable and adaptable. Novum Grafisk, Gothenburg.
54. Department of Basic Education, Presentation to the Parliamentary Portfolio Committee on Basic Education on the National Senior Certificate Examination of 2010, January 19, 2011.
55. Moloi, M. and Strauss, J. (2005) The SAQMEQ II project in South Africa: a study of the conditions of schooling and the quality of education, accessed April 7, 2011, available at http://www.sagmeq.org/links.htm. In the 1999, 2003, and 2011 TIMSS, South African students attained the lowest average test scores in both Mathematics and Science of all the participating countries.
56. Rossouw, J. P. (2010). Labour Relations in Education: A South African Perspective.2nd ed. Van Schaik: Pretoria at 114.
57. SAHRC (n 47 at12).
58. Section 10 of the South African Schools Act prohibits corporal punishment by anyone at a school.
59. Section 10.
60. SAHRC (n47 at 1).
61. Wolhuter, C. C., and Van Staden, J. G. (2008). Bestaan daar 'n dissiplinekrisis binne Suid-Afrikaanse skole? Belewenis van opvoeders. *Tydskrif vir Geesteswetenskappe* 48(3): 395.

62. *Christian Education South Africa v Minister of Education* (2000) (4) SA 757 (CC) at 786.

63. SAHRC (n47 at 13). The Human Rights Commission reported that corporal punishment is still applied in more than half of the schools (51.4 percent), with the Eastern Cape (65.3 percent), Mpumalanga (64.1 percent) and Limpopo (55.7 percent) reporting the highest incidences.

64. [2010] JOL 24847 (N).

65. SAHRC (n 47 at 13). During 2006, the Western Cape Education Department received ninety-four cases of which fifty-four were finalized by September 2006. The WCED stated that it has a 90 percent success rate in proving these cases. In most cases where the assaults were minor, the educators received fines together with a final written warning.

66. Mazengwe-Liwane, N. (2011) *Teacher unions and educator professionalism—An Education Law perspective.* MEd dissertation, North-West University.

67. Landman, W. (2011). Ethical, responsible leadership is far too rare. Sake 24 Beeld 4 February at p. 6.

68. Oosthuizen, I. J. (2007). Report on Learner Discipline in the Southern district, North-West Province. Platinum Press: Potchefstroom at 24.

69. Ibid.

70. Oosthuizen (n73 at 24).

71. Section 8A.

72. Hoexter, C. (2002). Administrative Law. In: Currie I and De Waal J (eds.) The new Constitutional and Administrative Law. Cape Town: Juta at 181.

73. Ibid.

74. Unreported Case no. 475/2007 (EC).

75. Botha, P., and Oosthuizen, I. J. (2009). A redemptive approach to school discipline. *Journal of Educational Studies* 8, 35–46.

76. [2005] JOL 15075 (N).

77. Currie, I., and De Waal, J. (eds.) The new constitutional and administrative law. Cape Town: Juta at 255.

78. 2004(1) SA 406 (CC).

79. Department of Education (2001) Regulations for Safety Measures at Public Schools. GN 1040 in GG 22754, Regulation 4(2).

80. Ibid.

81. Department of Education (n 92) Reg. 4(4).

82. Ibid.

83. Squelch, J. M. (1998). The establishment of new democratic school governing bodies: co-operation or coercion. In De Groof, J., Bray, E., Mothata, S., and Malherbe, R. (eds.) (1998). *Power Sharing in Education: Dilemmas and implications for Schools.*) Leuven: Acco., 101–13.

84. Powell NO v Van der Merwe [2005] 1 All SA 149 (SCA).

85. Department of Education. (1998). Guidelines for Consideration of Governing Bodies in adopting a code of conduct; s.4.5.1.

86. 2010 (5) SA 235 (GNP).

87. Van Vollenhoven, W. (2006). Learners understanding of their right to freedom of expression in South Africa, 70.

88. 2000 (4) SA 738 (WC).

89. 2008 (1) SA 474 (CC).

90. Pillay (n102 at para 44).

91. *Western Cape Residents' Association obo Williams and Another v Parow High School* (2006) (3) SA 542 (C).

92. Ibid at p.545 para B–C.

93. (2011) (3) SA 274 (CC).

Chapter Six

Reflections and Recommendations

Izak Oosthuizen, Charles J. Russo, and Charl C. Wolhuter

REFLECTIONS

An initial observation gleaned from the chapters in this volume and its companion book is that student misconduct presented significant challenges to educators all over the world. Moreover, dealing with learner misbehavior is so complex in its causes that new strategies are needed to address emerging forms of misconduct such as cyber-bullying. At the same time, the difficulties that student misbehavior cause in learning communities undoubtedly come at considerable cost both financially and to all involved.

The forms of student misconduct range dramatically from those that can be described as traditional and minor to those that are increasingly violent. Among the more common forms of misbehavior in just about all of the nations surveyed are students coming to class late, missing classes, leaving school without permission, truancy, improper attire and grooming, cheating on tests or examinations, not handing in work, neglect of academic work, disrespect toward teachers, open defiance and rudeness, forgery, disruptive behavior, obscene language, and using mobile phones without permission.

Serious offenses include fighting/assault, bullying (including cyber-bullying), physical or verbal threats, extortion and intimidation, theft and shoplifting, vandalism, substance abuse, smoking, sexual harassment of teachers or peers, and gang activities. Almost universally, since the use of technology in schools has grown dramatically and shows no signs of slowing down, it presents unique challenges. Yet, except for a dispute from South Africa involving cyber-bullying, technology was not identified as an emerging concern in schools in any of the other nations under consideration.

In the recent past a change has taken place in the conceptualization of the issue of student discipline in schools. To express this phenomenon in Weberian terms in dealing with student discipline, the attitude of educators has evolved from positional to charismatic to rational-legal authority. Further, a discernible international trend evident from the chapters in this volume is the shift toward a creed of human rights forming the parameter for dealing with student misbehavior.

Supporters of the Weberian perspective believe that methods for maintaining learner discipline should be humane. Under this approach, the object of maintaining learner discipline is to create school environments conductive for learning and teaching.

The imperative for sound discipline practices is frequently rooted in National Constitutions and Bills of Human Rights as well as international treaties. Such provisions pertain, for example, to the rights of learners not to be subjected disproportionately to severe treatments or punishment, not to be arrested or detained arbitrarily, and to be treated consistent with the observance of the principles of natural justice.

Student safety and security is a most important reason for a whole set of behavior rules. Under the common law doctrine of *in loco parentis*, literally, "in the place of the parents," educational officials have long had the legal duty to ensure that students are safe while in school. School authorities are thus vested with the power to preserve discipline to protect students, and themselves, from being the victims of misconduct while at the same time ensuring the teaching learning process continues smoothly.

The three founding values of the South African Bill of Rights, for instance, are equality, human dignity, and freedom. This Bill of Rights makes special provision for the right to freedom and security of the person, of religion, of belief and opinion, of expression, and association. In maintaining school discipline, all of these constitutionally entrenched rights, as well as the rights to education and administrative justice, rights also guaranteed by the Bill of Rights, should be respected, or at least weighed up against each other.

During the current age of globalization, the human rights base of preserving discipline in schools includes international conventions on Human Rights, such as the 1989 United Nation's Convention on the Rights of the Child,[1] as reflected in its Article 37,[2] protecting the child from being punished in cruel or harsh ways. Yet, not all signatories comply with these provisions.

It is exactly this creed of human rights which helped set the tone in the drive to abolish corporal punishment, traditionally one of the main, if not the primary, method of maintaining discipline in schools, in one country after the other. Among the nations covered in this volume, China, South Africa, and Turkey, corporal punishment in schools has been declared illegal. Where it is

looted and burned shops in the United Kingdom or the shootings in Columbine High School in Colorado and in Sandy Hook Elementary School in Newtown, Connecticut, in the United States.

On the other hand, school leaders in China, Malaysia, and Turkey, nations on the edge of human rights practices, have almost no problems with learner misconduct. The chapter on China reports their emphasis on the application of Max Weber's charismatic authority theories instead of the legally regulated approach. In terms of the Weberian perspective, dealings between students and teachers in China are defined in terms of that between a father and son.

The Weberian approach places the emphasis on relationships while elevating the status of the teacher to the respectable role of a parent. This also resonates in the traditional common law, the *in loco parentis* position of the teacher, a notion that seems to have fallen out of fashion in some Western democracies. However, the *in loco parentis* role of teachers is still strongly emphasized in Malaysia. The advantage of an emphasis on this theory is that it restores the respectful role to the position of teachers while enhancing a kind of intimacy between students and educators. Perhaps the most important aspect thereof is the fact that it restores the traditional role of authority and respect for the teacher in the eyes of the community.

Another key feature of the *in loco parentis* role of teachers is the duty of care, affording educators the obligation, and the authority, to ensure the safety of students. This duty affords teachers the authority to curb student misconduct if needed to enforce safe learning environments for all.

When all is said and done, it sometimes seems as if many of the Western countries embedded in a human rights dispensation are overly focused on the rights of the child. This emphasis was probably enhanced by international law. In this regard one should not underestimate the influence of international law instruments such as the 1989 UN Convention on the Rights of the Child. When compared to the 1959 UN Declaration of the Rights of the Child,[4] the former is much more progressive in promoting the individuality and interests of the children.

Surely, there cannot be any argument against the protection of the young and the best interest of the child. Yet, this approach can result in the paradoxical situation whereby it often appears that protecting the rights of students comes at the cost of teachers' status and authority.

The overprotection of students who misbehave is often detrimental to maintaining orderly teaching and learning environments. It could be that the pendulum of caring for student rights versus teacher authority has gone too far to the one side and needs a readjustment. Perhaps educators should seek to balance the scales in terms of affording teachers the authority to discipline learners who misbehave while simultaneously safeguarding student rights. As such, we offer the following recommendations in the hope of promoting discussion about what can work best in practice when safeguarding the rights of all members of school communities.

RECOMMENDATIONS

In light of the preceding analysis, educational leaders and lawyers not only in the nations reviewed in this volume but elsewhere should consider the following suggestions as forms of best practice when devising policies and practices addressing learner discipline.

First, leaders should ensure that teams charged with developing policies involve representatives of key constituencies, both when they are initially developed and when they are revised because ensuring cooperation is of paramount importance. Policy writing teams should include members of governing bodies, a school lawyer, administrators, teachers, staff, parents, community members, and learners, particularly at the upper levels since these policies would impact their activities.

Second, policies must include clear, precise definitions of prohibited student behavior such as bullying, intimidation, harassment, and other unacceptable behavior. Insofar as policies mandating punishment for such offenses as acting in a manner that is or saying something "mean" or "hurtful" can easily be invalidated as vague or over-broad, terms must be as precise as possible so that they can survive challenges and help to ensure school safety. Policies should add that off-campus misbehaviors can be punishable if they create hostile environments for victims, infringe on their rights, or create material and substantial disruptions to the educational process in school settings.

Third, policies should forbid physical, verbal, written, and electronic forms of misbehavior that might lead to physical acts of violence or gestures causing physical or emotional harm, damage to the property of victims, place victims in fear of harm, create hostile environments, or infringe on the rights of others.

Fourth, policies should prohibit misbehavior based on race, ethnicity, national origin, socioeconomic status, religion, gender, sexual orientation whether actual or perceived, or disabilities.

Fifth, policies should develop plans to protect victims from retribution and ridicule once they have filed complaints. Taking this step is important because a small but growing number of learners have committed suicide in response to being subjected to even more abuse from peers once they reported incidents to educators.

Sixth, policies must include substantive and procedural due-process protections that:

a. require students and staff to report instances of disciplinary infractions to designated school officials as soon as reasonably possible after they have occurred, such as by the end of a school day;
b. establish time frames within which administrators must complete investigations, typically ten school days, determining that educators may face liability for deliberate indifference by failing to respond to and investigate incidents;
c. protect the due process rights of the accused since allegations are just that—unless or until they are substantiated—and as such, policies should set deadlines by which time disciplinary processes must be completed, penalties imposed, and appeals filed and resolved while proceedings must be kept confidential;
d. specify a range of penalties for first, second, and repeat offenders from short-term suspensions to expulsions, adding that learners can receive significant sanctions even on their first offenses—if their actions warrant such discipline; and
e. mandate the reporting of incidents to law enforcement authorities if there is evidence that learners might have committed crimes.

Seventh, policies should be included in student and faculty handbooks. Also, learners and parents should be required to acknowledge in writing that they have read, understood, and agree to abide by these provisions in the handbooks.

Eighth, leaders should provide annual professional development opportunities for dealing with disciplinary problems for teachers and staff.

Ninth, leaders should offer programs for parents to help them better understand and respond to situations in which their children have either misbehaved or been harmed, due to the actions of their peers.

Tenth, leaders should offer counseling to victims and their families to help overcome the effects of being harmed by school violence.

Eleventh, educational leaders should develop peer-intervention or community-based programs such as those addressed in this book to help learners deal with misbehavior and violence in their lives.

Twelfth, teams should review their policies annually and not during or immediately after controversies to ensure that they are up-to-date with advances in the law, research, and worldview and life-view developments in the societies where they serve.

CONCLUSION

It is a reality of school life that students misbehave with the consequence that their actions often harm peers and ultimately themselves. Educators and lawyers can learn from other nations by identifying guidelines for dealing with similar cases while weighing them against the norms and value systems prevalent in the societies where they serve. Taking such a proactive approach just might help to make schools safe places where learning can actually occur.

NOTES

1. Available at http://www.ohchr.org/EN/ProfessionalInterest/Pages/CRC.aspx.
2. This article reads: Article 37 States Parties shall ensure that:

(a) No child shall be subjected to torture or other cruel, inhuman or degrading treatment or punishment. Neither capital punishment nor life imprisonment without possibility of release shall be imposed for offences committed by persons below eighteen years of age;

(b) No child shall be deprived of his or her liberty unlawfully or arbitrarily. The arrest, detention or imprisonment of a child shall be in conformity with the law and shall be used only as a measure of last resort and for the shortest appropriate period of time;

(c) Every child deprived of liberty shall be treated with humanity and respect for the inherent dignity of the human person, and in a manner which takes into account the needs of persons of his or her age. In particular, every child deprived of liberty shall be separated from adults unless it is considered in the child's best interest not to do so and shall have the right to maintain contact with his or her family through correspondence and visits, save in exceptional circumstances;

(d) Every child deprived of his or her liberty shall have the right to prompt access to legal and other appropriate assistance, as well as the right to challenge the legality of the deprivation of his or her liberty before a court or other competent, independent and impartial authority, and to a prompt decision on any such action.

3. 419 U.S. 565 (1975).
4. http://www.un.org/cyberschoolbus/humanrights/resources/child.asp

About the Authors and Editors

Izak Oosthuizen, PhD, taught high school for seventeen years before becoming an associate professor in Education Law on the Potchefstroom campus of the North-West University (NWU) in 1988. In 1999 he was promoted to professor. In 2011 he was appointed as a research professor in the Faculty of Education at the NWU Mafikeng campus and in 2014 was named Extraordinary Professor and Research Specialist. In 2004 Oosthuizen received the Senior Researcher award from the Education Association of South Africa. In 2005 and 2010 he was rated as an established researcher by the NRF. Since 1989 he has published about two hundred book chapters and articles related to Education Law.

Charles J. Russo, JD, EdD, is the Joseph Panzer Chair in Education in the School of Education and Allied Professions and adjunct professor in the School of Law at the University of Dayton, Ohio. The 1998–1999 President of the Education Law Association and 2002 winner of its McGhehey (Lifetime Achievement) Award, he is the author or coauthor of almost 250 articles in peer-reviewed journals and the author, coauthor, editor, or coeditor of fifty-two books. Russo has been the editor of the *Yearbook of Education Law* for the Education Law Association since 1995 and has written or coauthored in excess of 925 publications. He has spoken and taught extensively on issues in education law in the United States and in twenty-six other nations on all six inhabited continents. In recognition of his work in education law, Russo received an honorary PhD from Potchefstroom University, now the Potchefstroom Campus of North-West University, in Potchefstroom, South Africa, in May 2004.

Charl Wolhuter, DEd, is Comparative and International Education Professor at North-West University, Potchefstroom Campus, South Africa. Previously, he taught history of education and comparative education at the University of Pretoria and history of education and comparative education at the University of Zululand. He studied at the Universities of Johannesburg, Pretoria, South Africa, and Stellenbosch; he earned his doctorate in Comparative Education at StellenboschWolhuter; he has been guest professor at Brock University, Canada, Canterbury Christ University, UK, Bowling Green University and Mount Union University in Ohio, Driestar Pedagogical University, the Netherlands, and the University of Eastern Finland. Wolhuter is the author of books and articles in history of education and comparative education.

Irem Kızılaslan, PhD, is an instructor in the English Language Teaching Department at Dokuz Eylul University in Izmir, Turkey, where she completed her PhD. She has published in journals such as the *Journal of Ethnographic and Qualitative Research* and *European Journal of Teacher Education*. Her research interests are teaching English as a foreign language, teacher education, with special emphasis on teacher emotion, and qualitative research methodology.

Ricardo Lozano, PhD, is an assistant professor with the Educational Sciences Department at Yeditepe University in Istanbul where he teaches courses in comparative education, education and international development, educational leadership and planning, and educational management with an emphasis in organizational behavior. Ricardo is a graduate of Texas A&M University with a PhD in education administration and international economic development and a graduate of Concordia University, Texas, with a MEd in curriculum development and instruction. Lozano's main research interests are in the areas of comparative/international education along with education and international development.

Nina Beatriz Stocco Ranieri, PhD, is an associate professor in the Department of State Law of the Faculty of Law of the University of São Paulo (USP) and holder of the UNESCO Chair on the Right to Education. She is currently a member of the State of São Paulo Education Board. The author of the following books: *Autonomia Universitária* (*University Autonomy*), *Educação Superior, Direito e Estado* (*Higher Education, Law and the State*), and *Constitutional Aspects of the Right to Education, vols 1and 2*, among others, she has also written articles in the areas of Public Law and Education Law while contributing to law journals and other publications.

J. P. Rossouw, MEd, DEd, has twenty years of experience as a teacher and sixteen years as lecturer at the North-West University in Potchefstroom. A Professor in Education Law who specializes in Labour Law and Sport Law as applied to education he is the author or coauthor of sixteen books in Education Law and eighteen articles in peer-reviewed journals. He visited law schools and faculties of education, engaged in research in schools, and spoken at conferences in North America, Europe, Africa, and Asia. Rossouw is the National President of the SA Education Law Association (SAELA), member of the National Council of the Federation of SA Schools, and serves in the Exco of the Centre for Education Law and Policy.

Suping Shen, PhD, is a professor in the School of Education at Renmin University of China. Her research focuses on education law and policy. She has been the member of Standing Directory Board of Chinese Association of Educational Policy and Law. In addition, she participated in the drafting or amending of many educational bills and policies such as the Higher Education Act, Regulations on the Education of Persons with Disabilities, and National Medium and Long-term Educational Planning and Development Program.

Marius H. Smit, LLM, PhD, is an attorney, educator, and associate-professor in education law at the Faculty for Education Sciences at the North-West University, Potchefstroom. Editor of the book *Fundamentals of Human Rights and Democracy in Education: A South African Perspective*, he has authored articles in academic journals and chapters in books in education law. Smit is the National Secretary of the South African Education Law Association and serves on school governing bodies and the provincial committee of the Federation of South African School Governing Bodies.

Fatt Hee Tie, LLM, SJD, is a professor at the Faculty of Law, University of Malaya in Kuala Lumpur, Malaysia. Admitted as an advocate and solicitor to the High Court of Malaya in 1994, he taught in two secondary schools and a teacher training college for twelve years before joining the university. Besides teaching law and economics at Faculty of Law, he has taught education law for more than eighteen years at the Institute of Educational Leadership. He has published in the *Australia and New Zealand Education Law Journal*, *Education and Law Journal*, *International Journal for Education Law and Policy*, and *Education Law Journal*. He has also contributed chapters in education law books.

Jun Wang is an assistant research fellow of education law and policy in the Institute of Higher Education, Beijing Academy of Educational Sciences; he is also a PhD candidate of education economy and management in the School of Education, Renmin University of China.

Ran Zhang, PhD, is an associate professor of educational law in the Graduate School of Education, Peking University, China. She received an LLB from Peking University and a PhD in educational policy studies from Indiana University in 2009. She has published many articles and book chapters on Chinese or American educational law, and her dissertation won the Comparative and International Education Society Higher Education Special Interest Group Best Dissertation Award (2009–2010). She has received research grants from the U.S. National Science Foundation and Chinese National Social Science Foundation. Her research interests include educational law, comparative education, and research methodology.

www.ingramcontent.com/pod-product-compliance
Ingram Content Group UK Ltd.
Pitfield, Milton Keynes, MK11 3LW, UK
UKHW012042150926
475560UK00001B/153

9 781475 814828